The Age of the American Novel

Claude-Edmonde Magny

TRANSLATED BY ELEANOR HOCHMAN

Frederick Ungar Publishing Co.
New York

The Age of the American Novel

The Film Aesthetic of Fiction

Between the Two Wars

Translator's Dedication: *To David*

Translated from the original French, *L'Age du roman américain*, by arrangement with Editions du Seuil, Paris.

Pour Jean

Contents

CONCLUSION

Translator's Note

The Age of the American Novel is the first of Claude-Edmonde Magny's critical studies to appear in English. Published in 1948, it had been written during the three years following the Liberation of France, and its effect on French intellectuals was electric. Upon the reissue of the book twenty years later, critic R.-M. Albérès noted that this now classic work had both reflected and focused the literary preoccupations of a country emerging from an intellectual isolation only partly caused by the war and the Nazi occupation. With mixed emotions, attention understandably turned toward the United States, the "new, unknown, and incongruous country" that had become a leading world power. And from that country had come "a sort of raw and savage novel that seemed to have sprung from itself."

In both its insights and its occasional wrongheadedness, Mme Magny's analysis of the nature and message of this "American" novel—which was also being written in France—invites comparison with D. H. Lawrence's *Studies in Classical American Literature*. Lawrence rescued from the category of "juvenilia" a powerfully symbolic earlier literature that had come to be considered "just childishness," and he showed that it concealed profound truths about the American experience. Claude-Edmonde Magny's pioneering exercise in criticism took another "childish" art form—the movies—and demonstrated how it had inspired a new literary means of expression. Ellipsis, cutting, close-ups, long shots, in-depth focus, etc., were all shown to have generated literary equivalents, though Claude-Edmonde Magny's importance as a critic lies in her appreciation that cinematographic techniques are not stylistic gimmicks but the result of an author's ethical perception of experience. This concern with moral response can also be found in her *Précieux Giraudoux* (1945), *Les Sandales d'Empédocle* (1945), and *Histoire du roman français depuis 1918* (1950).

Much has happened in both the movies and the novel since the present study was first published, and unfortunately Mme Magny, who died in 1966, never returned to a consideration of many of the ideas contained in this work. That she was foresighted, however, can be seen by the fact that in speaking of the movies she stressed the importance of the director as *auteur* of the film. She saw—or foresaw—that we were "getting closer and closer to the time when the movie, like the novel, will unambiguously and unreservedly be attributable to one author"; and she predicted that theaters or film libraries would soon be projecting "the complete works of" René Clair, Fritz Lang, or Preston Sturges. In addition, many of Mme Magny's ideas point to the emergence of the "new novel," as exemplified by the works of Alain Robbe-Grillet, Nathalie Sarraute, and Michel Butor, as well as of the novel of "reportage," the best-known examples of which are Truman Capote's *In Cold Blood* and the latest works of Norman Mailer.

Though the major American authors discussed in this volume continued to write into the sixties, not one was to produce anything that equaled or surpassed the novels here analyzed, and Mme Magny's perceptiveness enabled her to foretell their development with often startling accuracy. Her chapters on Hemingway, Dos Passos, and Steinbeck were dazzling appreciations of their work up to the time in which she concluded her study, and she pinpointed their limitations and decline. A brilliant concluding chapter on Faulkner sees him as a writer whose work "surpasses that of all his contemporaries" because he sets down the conditions for a salvation "that must still be worked out and will always have to be rewon."

In the final analysis, the age of the American novel, as defined by Claude-Edmonde Magny, ended with World War II. The importance of this study is that it captures the immediacy of an existing period in American letters and relates it to the most popular—in both senses of the word—art of our time: the movies. It is not surprising that in reviewing a recent posthumous collection of her work *The Times Literary Supplement* (London) referred to Claude-Edmonde Magny as "one of the major French critics of this century," and noted that she was "one of the very few genuinely cosmopolitan critics her country has produced."

PART ONE

The American Novel
and the Movies

1 The Aesthetic of the Movies and of the Novel: A Comparison

For many years there has been much discussion about the influence of the American novel on the French novel, and it is certainly true that the technique of the French novel has undergone many modifications since the time French publishers refused the first part of Proust's À *la Recherche du temps perdu* (*Remembrance of Things Past*) on the grounds that it was too difficult to read. Without denying the direct influence Faulkner, Hemingway, and Joyce have had—and continue to have—on French writers, I would like to suggest another possible origin for this evolution of novelistic technique: the imitation, conscious or unconscious, of the techniques of the film, perhaps the common source for the changes that have taken place in both the American and the French novel. The situation would thus be one of a parallel evolution of the two literatures rather than of the influence of one on the other. The present study of this parallelism will be less a contribution to future literary study than an elucidation of some general aesthetic principles by means of a double comparison of both the French novel and the American novel, and of the novel and the movies.

If of all literary genres the novel is the one on which the film has had the most direct effect, it is because there is a triple relationship—psychological, sociological, and aesthetic —between them.

A superficial resemblance between these two genres is that they both address themselves to—and to a considerable extent attract—a mass audience, heterogeneous as to culture and class. (The ratio of novel readers to poetry readers is analogous to that between moviegoers and concert audiences.) Both novels and movies are considered fun, relaxation, "entertainment." Immediate pleasure is the first demand made of them; if there is anything else, it can come later. This is not true of poetry or concerts: the benefit derived from reading a poem or listening to a symphony obviously cannot be reduced to that of momentary pleasure. In short, within the area of literature—which is predominantly, like painting or music, an art reserved for the elite—only the novel, a genre of popular origin, is part of mass culture, whereas the cinema is perhaps the first example of an art whose very structure (no less than the economic servitude stemming from its technique) predestined it to be an art of the masses, the entertainment of those without leisure.

Psychologists tell us that pleasure results from the satisfaction of a need, and the deeper the need, the stronger the pleasure. If the novel and the film are equally capable of pleasing very large publics, and in a similar manner, it must be because they satisfy the same basic need—our desire to live a different life for a moment, to identify temporarily with the nature or emotion of another human being. In short, they satisfy man's curiosity about other men. They are "entertainments" because they take us out of ourselves for a while. This escapism is only the most banal, as well as the most negative, aspect of the quality known, when considered positively, as empathy. When we open a novel or enter a darkened movie house, we not only want to get out of ourselves and into some sort of abstract fairyland—if that were all we wanted, daydreaming, mathematics, chess, or drugs would remove us from real life just as well—but we also want to become someone else.

In the course of a book or a movie, we may feel this empathy first for one person and then for another—in Fritz Lang's *M*, for example, we feel in turn the fear of the victim and the anguish of the hunted criminal—or we may identify with an emotion rather than with an individual destiny—that is, we identify with the *anxiety* of two lovers searching for each other in the crowded railroad station and with their *disappointment* when they miss each other, rather than with the man and woman as such. The satisfaction of this "vicarious need" that makes us want to suffer or enjoy anonymously and pseudonymously (somewhat akin to the psychology of the voyeur) is not the least part of the psychological essence common to the two genres.

On the basis of this principle, one can explain most of the parallels in the psychology of novel readers and filmgoers. For instance, every publisher knows that short-story collections sell badly, regardless of the excellence of the individual stories and despite the virtues of the genre, amply evidenced by Maupassant, Pushkin, and Valéry Larbaud. Paul Morand had to publish *Magie noire* (*Black Magic*) as a novel; and authors like him, or like Marcel Aymé, who have found the short story their best form of expression, are nevertheless better known by the majority of readers for their novels—for *Champions du monde* (*World Champions*) or *La Jument verte* (*Green Mare*) rather than for *Europe Galante* (*Europe at Love*) or *Derrière chez Martin.*

The reason for this is exactly the same as the one that

explains the preference on the part of the rural population of the United States—those who go to the movies once a week either because they have no time to go more often or because there is only one movie house in the closest town—for series. By "series" I mean not so much serials[1] like *Les Misérables* or *Monte Cristo*, defined by continuity of plot, as films in which the same group of characters—like those in Chaplin or Mickey Mouse movies—constantly reappear (at least part of their popularity drawn from the familiar characteristics of these characters), or films like the Invisible Man series or the Nick Carter series. Each time a character like Judge Hardy, his son Andy (ritually played by Mickey Rooney), or Andy's fiancée or neglected girlfriend appears on the screen, the public is able to identify with him instantly and effortlessly; its pleasure is painless. In the same way, despite the acknowledged mediocrity of sequels to successful novels—from *Le Vicomte de Bragelonne* to *Little Men*[2]—there is an unending demand on the part of the public for the reappearance of its beloved characters. This is because it does not have to adapt to a new milieu, and the need to identify can be satisfied with the least expenditure of effort. Man is a creature of habit, and on opening a collection of seven or eight short stories, even the most enthusiastic and intellectual reader cannot help but evaluate the effort it will take to identify with a succession of seven or eight heroes instead of with only one.

[1] A very important distinction, without which one could explain the public's tastes for series solely by the fact that it does not have to assimilate new information about the characters, the plot, and so forth—in short, that it is spared (as is the author) the always disagreeable period of exposition. But in a series like that of the Hardy family (*Judge Hardy's Children, The Hardy Family on Vacation, Love Strikes Andy Hardy, Andy Hardy, Millionaire*)—or the Tarzan or Frankenstein family—there is continuity only in the characters created, and not in the plot.

[2] Sequel to Louisa May Alcott's *Little Women*. [*Le Vicomte de Bragelonne* is the third book of *The Count of Monte Cristo*.—Tr.]

The reader's tendency to identify the author of a book with the major character is well known. Victims of this unfortunate inclination (not always unreasonable) include Montherlant (with Costa, rebaptized Costal), Gide (first with Ménalque of *L'Immoraliste* [*The Immoralist*], then with Édouard of *Les Faux-Monnayeurs* [*The Counterfeiters*]), and Proust (with Marcel, the narrator of *À la Recherche du temps perdu*). There is a corresponding tendency on the part of moviegoers to identify, almost unconsciously, a star with his roles. They believe that Marlene Dietrich and Greta Garbo are "femmes fatales" even in real life, and they are scandalized by the fact that Mary Pickford, less innocent than on the screen, gets a Reno divorce in order to marry the handsome Douglas Fairbanks. The popularity of Bing Crosby and Irene Dunne was considerably diminished after they played scenes of drunkenness in *Sing You Sinners* and *Joy of Living*, respectively, and Ray Milland's publicity agent was very careful to insist on the complete teetotalism of the star of *The Lost Weekend*.

This is even more remarkable given the fact that there is no analogous tendency in the theater, which would seem on the surface to be more the artistic twin of the cinema than is the novel. The reason for this is that the psychological basis of the theater is not the spectator's identification with the hero: on the contrary, the aesthetic effect absolutely demands that the maximum possible distance between them be maintained. That is why Racine, in his prefaces, stresses temporal perspective or, failing that, spatial distance, as in *Bajazet*, and why Corneille uses the extraordinary—not to say legendary— nature of the action, the characters' high rank (which frees them from common, everyday problems), and all kinds of theatrical unreality to encourage the idea of tragic distance.

Indeed, while films are becoming more realistic, the theater is becoming ever more ritualized. Baty's marionettes;

the masks of *Les Mouches* (*The Flies*), which revive those of the ancient theater; Cocteau's alexandrines in *Renaud et Armide*; Montherlant's "lofty language" in *La Reine morte* (*Queen After Death*); Giraudoux's preciosity—these, to give only recent examples, are some of the manifestations of the theater's attempt to prevent any identification between spectators and characters by sharply separating the audience from the action represented. On the other hand, both the novel and the film systematically seek out all means leading to the emotional fusion of the character and the audience. An infinite number of plays can be—and many have been—written about the legends of Ariadne, Oedipus, the Atridae; it is unlikely that these themes would ever be used for a novel or a movie. The very grandeur of the characters, the aura of the fabulous that surrounds them, would disturb us. Drama, which has as its goal the representation of man as greater than nature, greater than himself, turns spontaneously to the buskin and the mask. The novel and the film, on the contrary, must lay bare the human heart and face.[3]

From among the many means the cinema has available to promote this identification between the spectator and the

[3] An apparent exception seems to be the vogue for historical and even mythical movies (like Fritz Lang's *Niebelungen* and Cocteau's *L'Eternel Retour* [*The Eternal Return*]—the failure of which is most likely due to the fact that it is a compromise between the basic mythic quality of the story and the superficial realism of the setting—and *La Belle et le bête* [*Beauty and the Beast*]). But we must not forget that the possibilities of identification vary with the culture and the milieu. Historical movies, for which Hollywood shows the same perverse predilection as some people have for costume balls, frequently disappoint the audience of midwestern farmers, who are only conscious of its strangeness. They also do not like foreign films, which do not allow them to become absorbed—in the strict sense of the word—because the language barrier constitutes too great an obstacle to assimilation. The overcultured accent of Katharine Hepburn disturbs them in the same way: it creates too great a social and cultural gulf between them and the actress.

protagonist, there is one in particular that directors have not hesitated to use—the continuation of the "type" created by such and such an actor, a type which, carried to its limit, becomes a character defined by the word "star," who transcends the different roles she plays. Americans carefully distinguish between the "leading lady"—the major female role in a movie—and the "star." Not everyone who wishes to become a star does so. It is not enough to be beautiful or to be a fine actress; it is not even enough to have a good publicity agent. What is indispensable is a collective consensus: an actress does not truly achieve the rank of star unless she has succeeded in so imposing her personality on the public that this personality is independent of the different things she may have to do in any given film; unless she has attained a unity over and beyond the diversity of her roles; unless, in short, the spectators see her as a type. We go to see a Garbo or Dietrich movie not because we are interested in the story of Queen Christina or a cabaret singer but because we want to see *them*, in exactly the same way that we go to see Chaplin in *his* films. Malraux has said it very well in his *"Esquisse d'une psychologie du cinéma"*: "A star is not, either from close up or far away, an actress who makes movies. A star is a person who has at least a minimum of dramatic talent and whose face expresses, symbolizes, incarnates, a collective instinct: Marlene Dietrich is not an actress like Sarah Bernhardt; she is a myth like Phryne."

An excellent interpretative artist like Bette Davis has never been able to raise herself to the level of "star," never—unlike Garbo, Chaplin, Mae West—been able to make crystallize around her a web of collective representations, precisely because she has too plastic a personality, too great a mimetic gift. She does not have an existence of her own but transforms herself completely from one film to another, truly *becoming* each of the new characters she plays. But Joan Crawford always has the same overlarge mouth and heavy jaw, and Katharine Hepburn always has the same prominent cheek-bones, vibrant personality, and Bryn Mawr accent. A large part of a good manager's job is to exploit intelligently the personality of the actress he is responsible for in such a way as to confer on her this permanence, this quality that transcends her roles.

This is no less true of the great novelists' efforts to give life to *their* characters. In those authors we generally think of as being the most novelistic, the transcendence by the hero of the specific situation he finds himself involved in corresponds to the transcendence of the star. We may forget the plot of *Vanity Fair* or *Pickwick Papers* (assuming there is one), but the figures of Becky Sharp, Sam Weller, or Mr. Pickwick continue to be sharp and gripping even after we have forgotten the circumstances of their lives. Vautrin, the Duchess of Maufrigneuse, and Mucingen exist independently of the adventures they have figured in. This quality of transcendence is especially marked in Balzac. Basically we know very little of certain secondary but constantly recurring characters of *La Comédie humaine* (*The Human Comedy*)—La Palférine, Marsay, the Marquise d'Espard, for example. Each of them occupies the center of at most one or two short stories, and when they appear in one of the novels, we do not learn much new about them. Yet they exist over and above our precise, enumerable information. They have a reality at least equal to that of real people we know and quite superior to what a knowledge of their psychology would confer. They partake of the same life, both mythic and concrete, as the classic figures of the screen. They are endowed with the same archetypal existence as Garbo's "femme fatale," Lillian Gish's ingenue, Jules Berry's somewhat mythomanic seducer. La Palférine, the Prince of Bohemia, exists outside the covers of *Béatrix* and *Un Homme d'affaires* (*A Man of Business*) exactly as

Dietrich exists outside *The Blue Angel* and Garbo outside *The Flesh and the Devil* or *Joyless Street.*

In addition, the characters of a novel are subject to the same contradictory conditions as the stars: they have to be simultaneously like us and "bigger" than us so that we may find in them an expanded self, free of its ordinary limitations, *exalted.* To launch a new star in America, one must confer on her *glamour*—that romantic prestige beyond beauty, sex appeal, or even charm, that intangible aureole thanks to which women will delight in seeing themselves in her and men in identifying themselves with her lovers. And all this must be done without denying her the characteristics that relate her to average human beings. She does not have to be beautiful, and certainly not with the kind of insolent beauty that would separate her too much from the spectator. The articles published about her will emphasize her moral qualities, those that everyone (theoretically at least) can acquire: physical pluckiness, courage in the face of adversity, simplicity, filial affection. Gary Cooper is described as preferring an old pair of gardening pants worn in one of his movies to all the clothes in his sumptuous wardrobe; William Powell, as selling his $250,000 house because it "intimidates" him; Clark Gable, as camping out.

The American critic Margaret Thorp, analyzing the ingredients that make a star, has said:

> If she is individual, the admired star need not be extravagantly beautiful. . . . In many ways it is an advantage for a star not to be too beautiful. She stands then closer to the average, and that is what the fans want: an ideal that they can emulate, one whose heights they might actually scale. . . . That is Janet Gaynor's great appeal: the little blonde from the typewriter who has exchanged her imitation lapin coat for sables, her Woolworth jewelry for real diamonds.[4]

[4] Margaret Farrand Thorp, *America at the Movies*, New Haven, Yale University Press, 1939, p. 71.—Tr.

No more plucked eyebrows or obviously dyed hair. The latest would-be star no longer strives to be a legendary princess but only the average young American girl who has known how to make the most of herself. The stars no longer try to hide the trivial details of their existence—their age, for example, or their pregnancy. When Lana Turner, one of the last glamour girls Hollywood tried to launch (so far without any great success),[5] had a baby, the studio decided to postpone the movie she was working on for a year. The cult of the natural is even more imperative when it involves young stars. We are told that Freddie Bartholomew has two dogs and adores swimming and football, and that when Shirley Temple was very young, though she had 250 dolls, she enjoyed making mudpies more than anything else.

Even culture has become a desirable attribute: Edward G. Robinson no longer has to hide his collection of modern paintings; William Powell is photographed in his library; Merle Oberon's bedroom is lined with filled bookshelves; Paulette Goddard arrives in Paris and her husband, Burgess Meredith, cables her a choice of birthday presents—a large Picasso or a small Renoir. (It is true that he has the reputation of being the "most intellectual actor in Hollywood"—noblesse oblige!) And finally, to top it all, it seems that Deanna Durbin reads as many as thirty books a year (though we are not told which). The social and humanitarian preoccupations of the stars, and even their political opinions, are openly discussed. In other words, according to current publicity practices, every conceivable means is used to humanize the stars, to bring them down to the level of the public. It is for this reason that the young leading men are rarely extraordinarily handsome: Cary Grant, Clark Gable, and Robert Montgomery are far from having perfect features. What they do have (in addition

---

[5] Written in 1945.

to their talent as actors, which is not in question here) is an air of health that seems as if it could be acquired by anyone who exercised regularly at the YMCA. The fan magazines systematically support this process of identification between the spectator and his idol. Thanks to them, the admirers of Corinne Griffith or Veronica Lake can dress like their heroine, eat the same foods, possibly (if, for example, they win some contest) wear a bracelet or a negligee that has previously belonged to her. The recurrence of the Cinderella myth in the movie magazines lends itself to similar interpretation. On the one hand, there are endless stories about the misery of Hollywood extras and statistical evidence about the number of people necessarily doomed to failure. On the other hand, they continue to tell how Joan Crawford began as a salesgirl and Clark Gable as an extra, how James Cagney worked as an elevator operator for thirteen dollars a week and Olivia de Havilland was discovered by a talent scout while she was acting in a high-school play, how . . . Famous actors have arrived (the legend tells us) not because of exceptional qualities but thanks to a combination of luck and courage possible to anyone. Thus the cinema magnifies—"glorifies," as they say—the actor or actress and tries to make of him an ideal being, an archetype whose life appears enviable to every spectator; but at the same time it concretizes this ideal and tries to bring it down to the level of average humanity insofar as this is compatible with the star's prestige.

This is equally true of the novel. More handsome than the reader, more brilliant, capable of living out destinies infinitely more sensational, the characters in a novel must nevertheless remain similar enough to that reader for an imaginary identification to take place. The author will therefore try to individualize them as much as possible by means of specific characteristics, for the more abstract the character of a novel is, the more difficult it is for us to recognize ourselves in him.

Because he is so disincarnate, Valéry's Monsieur Teste is not a novelistic character; he is so abstract that he seems barely human, and we cannot manage to project our own feelings or thoughts onto him. Inversely, an actor's publicity will emphasize his most individual peculiarities, manias, superstitions —all the absurd or moving qualities that endear a person to us: Jean Harlow's passion for oysters, someone else's tendency to freckles or fear of the number thirteen. The vamps must especially guard against becoming too mythical. Thus, we know that the gaunt-cheeked Marlene loves good meals (and is not afraid of getting fat) and that Garbo (the haughty princess of legend) always wears an old raincoat when she goes out.

By what is only *apparently* a paradox, the hero of a novel, like the star, must not be too universal, too depersonalized, too abstract; every kind of man should be able to identify with him. What kind of novel is it when we do not know if the heroine is blonde or brunette? Authors of detective stories are well aware of this and carefully differentiate their detective—that is, the "sympathetic character" through whose eyes the reader will see the action and whose point of view he will adopt—from the common run of mankind by means of small oddities that are almost caricatural: Sherlock's violin, pipe, and cocaine (to say nothing of his dressing gown); Poirot's Belgian accent, gallicisms, and artful simplicity; Lord Peter Wimsey's monocle, fortune, Oxford accent, and wine expertise; and Nero Wolfe's obesity, orchids, misogyny, and laziness. The list is almost endless. This is, of course, rather schematic, but a hero that is a caricature is preferable to one that is too abstract. On the screen, as in a book, we thirst for concrete details about the characters because aesthetic identification is possible only with individuals. A character in a play, however, exists most forcefully when he is most stylized; all tragedy is classical because the theater is essentially impersonal.

The parallelism between the novel and the film may be carried still further in terms of the history—that is, the evolution—of the two genres. There is absolutely no doubt that the movies are undergoing a "star crisis": the latest Hollywood launchings, from Lana Turner to Greer Garson, do not seem to have been crowned by success. There are good actresses, or popular actresses—like Rosalind Russell, Vivien Leigh, and Michele Morgan—but even their most fanatic admirers would not be able to credit them with the transcendence over their specific roles that characterizes the star. Joan Fontaine and Ingrid Bergman have cinematic personalities that have been developing continuously for several years, but neither of them has been an overwhelming sensation on the order of Mary Pickford or Greta Garbo—or even of Joan Crawford, queen of the jazz age. For a moment there were hopes for Veronica Lake, but I am afraid she was only a brushfire. In France, Odette Joyeux is the only one who always has the same job in her films—a job that is quite indefinable but basically consists of "being Odette Joyeux," whether it be in films that are average (*Entrée des Artistes*), poor (*Les Petites du Quai aux Fleurs* or *Sylvie et le fantome*), or excellent (*Le Marriage de Chiffon* and the adorable *Douce*). Perhaps the Dietrich of ten years ago was the last star.

The reasons for this disappearance of stars are mysterious, and they are quite likely of a sociological nature. In the life of societies there are undoubtedly periods when the collective consciousness is integrative and others when it is disintegrative. A star being the incarnation of a powerful collective instinct, the convergence of desires implied by her appearance is probably only possible during periods that are relatively stable, or at least strongly cohesive. Everything leads us to believe that we are instead living in a period of transformation and disintegration. This may well be a wild hypothesis. The important fact is that this growing scarcity of stars is paralleled by what is happening in the detective story (the genre that is more sensitive than any other to sociological fluctuations because it is—or at least it is considered to be, and that comes to the same thing—less literary, less "lofty," and therefore less at the mercy of individual initiative or genius, and a more faithful register of collective transformations). There is an analogous disappearance of the detective endowed with sensational or *glamorous* characteristics, like the blind Max Carrados, Chesterton's priest, Father Brown, the foreign Hercule Poirot, the drug-taking Sherlock, the aristocratic Peter Wimsey, or even the tinged-with-homosexuality Nero Wolfe.

In the latest English mysteries the detection is entrusted to insignificant personalities, to dull, lifeless, colorless characters who are often interchangeable from one book to another and who are even very often—and how the shades of Arsène Lupin and Raffles, gentleman-thief and thief-gentleman, must shudder—connected with the official police (for reasons of verisimilitude, dare say their creators!). Even in the "American-style" stories of James Hadley Chase or Raymond Chandler,[6] where the detective is presented as the toughest of toughs and where we consequently expect a somewhat colorful human being, we are most often given nothing but gray policemen who are pale copies of Hammett's Ned Beaumont or Sam Spade (with here and there a light sprinkling of Perry Mason), quite indistinguishable from the criminals they track.

In other words, the neutral detective without personality,

[6] I except Peter Cheney's excellent Lemmy Caution, but only in his first appearances, for after the fourth volume he became as monotonous and irritating as S. S. Van Dine's Philo Vance (of unhappy memory) in his fifteenth volume.

like Commissaire Maigret, is taking over, in England as in France, from the detective like Sherlock Holmes or Arsène Lupin because of a phenomenon that can be related to the current crisis of the novel. In recent detective stories, the hero merges into the story and more and more tends to melt into it. In short, he is in the process of abdicating from his transcendence just as the star is disappearing from the film in favor of the actress.

The film and the novel thus operate on the same psychological principle; they offer their devotees the same kind of pleasure, based on the satisfaction of an identical need. The aesthetic pleasure offered the spectators of a play is, on the contrary, quite different. Because of this, the physical conditions in which we view both the film and the play are—despite their apparent similarity—also completely different. Between the playhouse and the movie house there is only a superficial analogy; the two locations have only the word "house" in common.

The film public and the novel public do, however, constitute social groups having the same structure. When Roger Caillois, in *Puissances du roman*, insists on the individual nature of the novel, an individual nature deriving from the very conditions under which it has to be read—that is, from the kind of isolation in which it automatically places the reader—everything he says, however unlikely it may seem, applies equally well to a movie. When we think of a man in the process of reading a novel, the image that comes to mind is that of a solitary being in an empty room, imprisoned by the narrow circle of light from his lamp; we see him as a creature lost in a vision created by his reading, hypnotized by that vision, and restored by it to his fundamental solitude. This is just as true of the cinema, though the fact is ordinarily hidden by the material conditions in which movies, for reasons that are partly technical, partly economic, are currently viewed.

For the production of a film to be a profitable business enterprise, it is necessary that it be seen by a large number of people who have paid admission to sit together in a movie house. But let television be perfected, let production adjust itself to this technical improvement, and the film will recover its basic essence. At that time, when it again becomes like the novel in all ways, it will, like the novel, address itself to those things that are deepest and most solitary in man. We have all gone to the movies with a friend—someone who is as close and familiar to us as can be—and we all know how unsatisfactory an experience it is in terms of sharing or exchanging ideas. Intimacy, and even simple communication, comes to a complete halt as soon as the story begins to unfold; as the first image appears on the screen, each person returns to the solitude of his own perception, emerging from it for at most a few brief seconds in order to exchange a couple of words that are abruptly cut short for fear of losing the thread of the dialogue. The interchange between the two spectators is even less than if they were reading the same book at the same time, for the movie does not wait; it is not, like a novel, always at our disposition, and our conversation would distract from the words being spoken on the screen.

There is still another aspect of this same truth: everyone knows that to see the eight hundredth performance—or a provincial performance—of a play one might have enjoyed early in its run or in Paris is to court almost certain disaster. More generally, one's feeling about a play depends to a great extent on the ambiance of the theater (I can remember having laughed at some less than mediocre comedies simply because the public, which had come to be amused, was exploding into contagious laughter at each retort). It is incomparably easier for a moviegoer to retain his independence; a claque has never been able to freeze out a good film or impose a bad one, as it is able to do with plays. The films I remember having been most moved by were those seen or reseen in the anonymity of a small neighborhood movie house two or three years after they had created a furor in the first-run houses, and neither my tears nor my laughter was disturbed by the stupid comments of my neighbors or by the boos that may have greeted an unusual approach that struck me as fine.

Emotional contagion is minimal at the movies, maximal at the theater. In a movie house it is as if the two arms of our seat and the surrounding darkness (and especially the powerful magic of the images on the screen) are enough to protect us from everything that is not the story, to make us withdraw into ourselves. Our memories of a playhouse are of an audience powerfully united by laughter, by boredom, or by enthusiasm, but if we try to remember the reactions of a movie audience (and it requires an effort to remember this, because while these reactions impose themselves on us at the theater, they escape us at the movies), what we remember is the feeling of a *divided* house—of half-consciously heard comments, or of our neighbors' reactions, none of which impinges to a great extent on our own pleasure or alters the quality of it. Even laughter is less infectious at the movies than at the theater. The audience watching *Here Comes Mr. Jordan* laughed very often, but *its* laughter did not make *me* laugh at those passages I found moving or profound. I repeat, it is incomparably easier to maintain one's freedom of judgment in a movie house than in a playhouse.[7]

The fundamental reason for this difference is that the movie is only slightly—or not at all—a spectacle; it is much more—like the novel—a story. The aesthetic essence of the theater is spectacle, that is, something that can be simultane-

[7] For other arguments supporting this same thesis, see Albert Laffaye's remarkable article in *Les Temps Modernes* (No. 5).

ously apprehended by thousands of persons forming a community to such an extent that the perception of each one conditions that of the others and even that of the perception of the audience as a whole. The movie, however, is perceived individually by each of the spectators in his own way. The theater's basic aim, which has remained the same since the time of the Greek tragedies and the medieval mysteries, is to re-create for at least a moment the collective soul, to re-form (by secular means) a community (even if not a society) by securing the convergence of attention of everyone united by this participation. The dramatic scene is perceived at the same time by all the spectators; and because of its rigid, objective structure, it is the same scene that is imposed on them all. On the other hand, many people see a movie in the same way as they listen to music or read a novel: by projecting their personal dreams and aspirations onto the scenes unfolding before them, as if the screen (like the symphony, like the novel) were only a point of departure, a support for the imagination. Speak to any of the spectators leaving a movie and you will find that they did not perceive the film as a work external to themselves, endowed with an independent existence, but as the very stuff of their dreams—materialized, enriched, made incarnate.

This is undoubtedly why the film, like the novel, is an art form so exactly suited to the modern consciousness and its needs. This is partly because of its polymorphism, of course, but even more because it so exactly embodies what distinguishes contemporary society from a more primitive society: the simultaneously particular and personal relationship of the individual to the collective soul in the former, as opposed to that individual's more diffuse participation in the community in the latter. With the same danger: the barely conscious descent into absolute solitude and the loss of all objectivity by the substitution of what one wants for what actually *is*—in short, the concrete equivalent of the attitude philosophers call solipsism. Modern man is alone in a movie house, though he is surrounded by a thousand spectators similar to himself. They too are lost in their own dreams, they too are hypnotized by the screen and what is happening on it—but each is for the moment a stranger to the others. One thousand consciousnesses become impervious to their neighbors, divided by what seems to unite them. The movie each of these beings sees is *his* movie, not the one the director made, just as the novel he reads is *his* novel, not the one Mauriac or Colette actually wrote. He is alone, as each man listening entranced to the Arabian storyteller is alone, face to face with his dream incarnated in Sinbad or Scheherazade.

We thus arrive at the most basic relationship between the novel and the film—the *aesthetic* relationship that is the foundation for the more superficial psychological or sociological resemblances: both are narratives. Now the narrative has its own laws, and these are quite different from those of the spectacle. One of its fundamental requirements is continuity, the characteristic that is so clearly evident in every series of stories passed down to us by oral tradition—*The Arabian Nights*, for example. Far from being the result of an initial arbitrary decision that is later preserved because of tradition, most novelistic conventions, as well as most of the usual techniques of the film, can be explained by the need to preserve at all costs the continuity which is constantly being threatened by the very richness of the material that must be integrated into a narrative made ever more complex by the development of the art.

Among other things, the following chapters will show how right the modern novel has been to borrow from the cinema those narrative techniques that help strengthen this continuity—for example, the use of rapid shifts from long

shots to close-ups and vice versa, or of lap dissolves. Until the
end of the nineteenth century, the most common means of
assuring the continuity essential to the novel was to use a narrator (sometimes one identical with the hero, as in Eugène
Fromentin's *Dominique* or Jean Schlumberger's *Un Homme
heureux*; sometimes someone else, a secondary character, like
Lockwood in *Wuthering Heights*). In other words, interposed
between the narrative and the audience was a consciousness
whose job it was to "report." The film does the same thing
through the use of the camera lens, a retina on which everything must register. It is therefore both normal and surprising
(surprising because it would seem superfluous) that the film
too has recently felt it necessary to make use of the subterfuge
of a narrator—that is, to interpose an additional lens between
the creator and his public.

This is only one of the most striking—as well as one of
the most recent—examples of the constant crossfertilization
that exists between two arts continuously exchanging procedures, and it confirms what we have said about their deep
relationship. Such innovative details, even those particular to
a given director, demonstrably add to the parallelism between
the novelistic and the cinematic narrative (perhaps without
the user even being aware of it). Thus Sartre, otherwise se-
vere in his treatment of Orson Welles's technique, is unable to
refrain from citing what he describes as Welles's use of "foreshortenings that generalize" in *Citizen Kane*. Of this film,
Sartre says:

> There is a curious attempt to give certain images the quality
> of the frequentative. We say, in effect, "He keeps forcing
> his wife to sing on every stage in America," which condenses
> in one single phrase a number of events that happened day
> after day. . . . Welles excels in this kind of foreshortening
> that generalizes . . . the method is a well-known one. But
> until now it served, on the fringes of the action, to show

political opinion or the influence of an action on the collectivity, or even merely as a transition. In *Citizen Kane* it is
part of the *action*, it *is* the action; it is the essence of the
story, and the specific, dated scenes are, on the contrary, the
exception. It is as if the narrator were saying, "He used to
make her sing everywhere; she was upset by this; once she
tried to tell him so. . . ."

Even more significant is the current tendency[8]—so
marked that it has struck all the critics—for every movie,
from no matter what country or even what year, to be expressly made as a first-person narrative instead of as a succession of objective images photographically reproduced. The
cinema is developing in the direction of the narrative to the
point of borrowing from the novel its most specific and most
traditional methods of narration—those that contemporary
writers readily acknowledge to be slightly old-fashioned if
not completely out-of-date. From this point of view the most
remarkable film—the one that truly uses the first-person narration in a hyperbolic fashion—is the extraordinary *Lady in
the Lake*, directed by actor Robert Montgomery. In this movie
the camera is constantly in the place of the hero, showing us
things as they appear to him, without our ever being allowed
to see him except when he looks at himself in a mirror. This is
not a new idea: Orson Welles wanted to make *Heart of
Darkness* this way even back in 1940. He had to renounce the
project because the producers were afraid of such daring.
What is new in Montgomery's film is the extreme consistency
and methodicalness of its realization.

Though they do not go so far as *Lady in the Lake*, in the
past year there have been a great number of movies in which
either there is a narrator whose commentary constantly under-

[8] This is being written at the beginning of 1947. In the remarkable
fourth issue of *Revue du Cinéma*, the tendency here noted was analyzed and discussed by almost every critic, and I am indebted to this
source for several of the following suggestions.

lines the images and who is none other than the hero—and
which thus make use of what has been called the "first-person
voice"—or in which, at a crucial moment of action, we completely identify with the vision of the main character. In
The Lost Weekend, where delirium tremens induces hallu-
cinations, the whole sequence during which the bat flutters
and enlarges on the wall could be paralleled by Benjy's
monologue in Faulkner's *The Sound and the Fury:* in both
cases the problem is to introduce us into a world of madness
incommunicable by logical narration, the disorder of which can
only be transmitted to us by an implacable fidelity to the perception, no matter how incoherent, of the character who lives
in that world. Sacha Guitry had already employed first-person
narration in *Roman d'un tricheur (The Story of a Cheat),* but
only in certain places and in an equivocal fashion: he occasionally appeared on the screen and watched himself act, so
to speak, instead of remaining the invisible narrator, as he
should have done. The direct narrative thread was thus
abruptly broken; one left "the domain of vision for that of
illustration."[9] On the other hand, in *Double Indemnity* the
method is employed with perfect consistency. The unfolding
of the narrative is accomplished by the murderer's confession
into a dictaphone; this marks all the other events with a seal
of fatality, since we know in advance that they will result in
the crime. Superficially, *Brief Encounter* uses the same technique, but it has a completely different significance. What is
important here is not Laura Jesson's explicit confession to her
husband but her interior monologue, the phrases she murmurs
to herself while reliving her story. Here the point is to obtain
from the spectator—from the beginning to the end of the
story—a total sympathy for, and a complete identification
with, the heroine.

    [9] Jacques Doniol-Valcroze, "Naissance du véritable ciné-oeil," *Revue
du Cinéma,* p. 28.

The aesthetic effect of the first-person narration is evident. With it, we break with the film spectator's hitherto impersonal—as well as false and abstract—vision, and arrive at an apprehension that more closely approaches the normal conditions of perception. This signals the end of the new style of humanity created by the first developments of cinematic technique—that is, "the man in the dark room," omniscient and in a way depersonalized, plunged objectively into *stories* he has not experienced and is not experiencing, able to take the place of each character in succession, finding it normal to see a certain number of spectacles of the world that he would never see otherwise, not because they are absurd or impossible but because in ordinary life his ways of seeing and hearing would be completely different.[10] At the same time the narrative acquires a greater persuasive value; it has the same force as the testimony of the witness who comes to the front of the courtroom and says, "I saw . . ." or "This is what happened to me." (This effect was discovered in radio—that disembodied art par excellence—by Orson Welles in the course of his excellent Mercury Theater programs.) Thanks to first-person narration, the spectator is not outside the story; he really *lives* it, by identifying with one other person, once and for all, without those oscillations of attention and sympathy that were previously centered on first one and then another character at the whim of the movements of the camera—a method that made for a considerable waste of emotional force.

At the same time, by becoming subjective, the narration gives the director much greater freedom with time. This was already quite apparent in Marcel Carné's *Le Jour se lève* (*Daybreak*), though in this case the subjectivity of the narrative derives from the actual scenario and not from a special narrative mode. When the movie begins, we see Jean Gabin

[10] Ibid., p. 26.

in a furnished room, besieged by the police; flashbacks are then used to explain the circumstances that have brought him there. From time to time the camera inexorably brings us back to this miserable room in which the hero is feeling himself ever more trapped: the action of the movie derives from what he remembers. With this film the cinema—until now riveted to the expression of that "eternal present" which is, as Albert Laffaye has so well demonstrated,[11] its own specific time—has truly conquered the past.

This insertion of a story that has already happened into a violent story that *is happening*—a very old procedure in the novel, but one that may nevertheless seem completely fresh under special circumstances[12]—is to be found in many other recent movies: *Brief Encounter* offers the same oscillation from the present to the past; *The Magnificent Ambersons* is "written" entirely in the past by the voice of Orson Welles, who tells the story and "subtitles" the images as they unfold; *Citizen Kane*'s story is also told in flashbacks; and finally, the extraordinary (and admirable) *Dead of Night* rests on the hypothesis that neither the hero nor the spectator can distinguish between dream and reality, present and past.[13] One might say that with the first-person narrative the cinema has finally freed itself from its long servitude to the problem of time—or at least of time as it is usually represented: linear and irreversible. It can now define time as other than the one-dimensional *continuum* it is conceived of as by the collective consciousness. The camera, as if it were moved by H. G. Wells's time machine, can now place itself in front of, behind,

[11] In the previously cited article in *Les Temps Modernes*.

[12] Witness Hemingway's short story "The Snows of Kilimanjaro," where flashbacks are used with the frequency and audacity that are undoubtedly the prerogative of writers very sure of their craft.

[13] And I do not even mention such films as *Farewell, My Lovely*, which merely use a technique borrowed from *Double Indemnity* without that technique having any intrinsic significance.

or within this continuum. The film seems to have had to borrow from the novel a method that would give it the freedom to go backward, that would allow it to share the novel's long-enjoyed ability to "reverse the engine."

At the same time, other innovations are completing this liberation. All the critics have commented on the daring depth of field that Orson Welles—aided by the skill of his cameraman Gregg Toland and the invention (purely technical) of the pan-focus lens—used in *Citizen Kane.* Very few of them tried to understand its significance, and many criticized it as a kind of showing off, a use of novelty for its own sake. The same effects are to be found in *The Magnificent Ambersons;* and in *Great Expectations,* the English director David Lean (who also did *Brief Encounter*) makes masterly use of the technique. The consequences of this new method of film construction (for with it the architectural film succeeds the narrative film and simultaneity succeeds simple sequence, just as in the novel *La Comédie humaine* succeeds *Adolphe,* and *Ulysses* succeeds *Tono Bungay* or *Tess of the D'Urbervilles*) have been carefully discussed by André Bazin,[14] who analyzes two or three extremely pertinent examples of this new kind of movie (an analysis we unfortunately cannot reproduce here) and examines its significance.

Previously, the camera "analyzed" a scene and broke it up into a certain number of "shots" that it offered to the sympathetic attention, the *Einfühlungsvermögen,* of the spectator; the labor of perception and aesthetic identification was done in advance for the spectator by those responsible for the cutting and editing. Without the spectator being aware of it, his interest was automatically caught by the significant details. When Orson Welles films a dramatic scene, he lays its elements before us *simultaneously* and makes *us* do the work of

[14] "La Technique de Citizen Kane," *Les Temps Modernes,* No. 17, pp. 942–49.

breaking up the scene—work that previously the director had obligingly spared us. When Kane's wife tries to commit suicide, we see (or we should be seeing, for the director works for the ideal spectator just as the author writes for the perfect reader) all the composite parts of the scene, from the glass and spoon in the foreground to the sound in the extreme background of Kane vainly calling out and hitting the door with his shoulder. In *The Magnificent Ambersons*, when Mary breaks with George Amberson, the street in which the scene takes place is completely visible at every moment because of the extreme clarity with which the background is photographed, and this street is as important as the actual byplay of the actors. What Orson Welles places before us at every moment is a complete fragment of the universe, a microcosm in which all the elements are equally necessary, equally important, and in which each one derives an added intensity from the presence of all the others. Welles's *synthesizing* point of view restores to us a world of density, in which each object is indispensable and has its own function and meaning.

And that, of course, is the very essence of the specific aesthetic of the film, the object of which, as was so ably demonstrated by Albert Laffaye, is to produce in us the illusion that everything in the universe, man and things alike, is united in a close solidarity and that each object is connected to all the others in a complete system of reciprocal dependence, from which it derives its own existence. This is like the world of simultaneous copresence so well evoked by Jean Wahl (following Whitehead and even Heidegger)—a world in which all objects know one another and in which nothing exists that does not perceive everything else and is not perceived by everything else, as suggested by Bergson in the first and extraordinary chapter of *Matière et mémoire (Matter and Memory)*. The characteristic art of Orson Welles thus seems the very hyperbole of the film aesthetic, and this aesthetic is itself pregnant with an implicit metaphysic whose agreement with the intuitions of the most recent philosophical systems should not surprise us.

Purely from the point of view of the effect produced on the spectator, a scene (such as the ones I have cited from *Citizen Kane* or *The Magnificent Ambersons*) can obviously gain in dramatic intensity when represented entirely by means of foreshortening (a foreshortening very different, despite the similarity of the word, from the generalizing foreshortenings of which Sartre spoke). The technique of linking scenes taken at different depths of field, and the technique of traveling shots—each of which did the spectator's job by undertaking for him the disagreeable task of interpretation imposed on the reader by even the least complicated novel—had cut the cinema off from one of its possible dimensions, the one it has in common with painting: simultaneity. The discovery of cutting *temporalized* the cinema by allowing it for a time to evade its spatial possibilities; this was a revolution analogous to that of impressionism, which certainly renewed the art of painting, but at the cost of the loss of that absolute clarity of background so striking in the Italian primitives and, even more, in Breughel's "Fall of Icarus" or his "Spring" (in the series known as *The Four Seasons*).

It is noteworthy that at the same time as the film, with no doubt overweening ambition, is trying to escape from the pure narrative and break out of its old grooves, the novel also seems, with Dos Passos and Joyce, to have a parallel ambition: to escape from the linearity with which it was apparently cursed by its material conditions of perception and to strive for the simultaneity of polyphonic music or painting. Like the "dramatic blocs" of Orson Welles, which are however intersected and supported by a more classically linear narrative, the novelistic prose of Joyce tries to give us a synoptic view, a simultaneous perception of the consciousness of various characters; the film, of course, in conformity with its point of view, presents us with the simultaneity of their different behaviors. At the same time, Joyce tries to give us the interpenetration of present and past, which his belief in the "unconscious" authorizes him to seek technical expression for.

The major objections to Orson Welles are: the difficulty, not to say impossibility, for the average spectator (especially since he has been brought up with habits of extreme laziness) of distinctly perceiving three shots simultaneously rather than one; the necessity for close collaboration with the director (at least equal to that which reading demands of the reader) and the good will this calls for; the extreme fatigue that is the inevitable result of this; and the necessity of seeing the movie more than once in order to understand it completely (what reader can boast of having immediately and thoroughly understood *À la Recherche du temps perdu* or *Ulysses*, or even *La Chartreuse de Parme* [*The Charterhouse of Parma*] or *Les Liasons dangereuses*, which are on the surface so much more simple and linear?). These are the same objections that were made against Proust, Joyce, and Dos Passos and are still being made today.

Till now, film has been (voluntarily) an art even more *analytic* than those using language; with the discovery of depth of field (which, if it corresponds, as I think it does, to something truly profound, will certainly become the basis of a "school"), we are moving toward a *synthesizing* cinema (at least to the same extent as modern painting or music). It remains to be seen if the "message" of Welles's films will compensate even the well-disposed spectator for the effort he will have to put forth. One may well ask if the creator of *Citizen Kane* and *The Magnificent Ambersons* will ever have something to say in his movies about anything other than the drama of pride and the will to power—and the despair and solitude that are the punishment thereof. In other words, will he ever do anything but autobiographical films, and will these films ever have a spiritual reality and human significance proportionate to their technical perfection and the difficulty of understanding them? But this is the same objection that can be made to Joyce's *Finnegans Wake*, where the message of *Ulysses* (already rather thin) seems to have become even slighter in proportion to the extent that the author's technical preoccupations became more demanding—and perhaps also became a barrier to his further progress along the path of wisdom.

Another tendency that shows the relationship between the latest developments of the movies and the novel should also be mentioned. One of the obvious differences between the two art forms is that one is collective, the other individual: a movie—like poetry, according to the surrealists—is made by everyone (or at least by a great many people), not by one person. Without counting the actors or the many technicians of varying importance (from the cameraman to the editor, and including the set designers and the costume designers), or even the financiers or the producer, the essential responsibility has heretofore rested (at least since the advent of sound) on the shoulders of two men: the director and the scriptwriter. It is impossible, for example, to minimize Jacques Prévert's contribution to the films of Marcel Carné, and one can as easily define the constants of Prévert's art[15] as analyze the universe of Jean Renoir or John Ford.

As a reaction against this duality, strong-minded directors are more and more tending to unite in their own person the diverse functions previously filled by different individuals: in *Citizen Kane*, Orson Welles is director, scriptwriter, and principal actor; in *The Magnificent Ambersons*, he is director,

[15] As Roger Leenhardt did with such great success in an article in *Fontaine*.

adapter, and narrator. To make *Lady in the Lake,* actor
Robert Montgomery (while listening to himself and even
watching himself through the intermediary of a mirror) assumes the role of director—to say nothing of cameraman, since
it is he who points the camera, which incarnates the narrator's
consciousness, on the other actors! Preston Sturges, who began
as a writer, is now responsible for the filming of his own
scripts. Charles Brackett and Billy Wilder, both scriptwriters
at first, now form a team in which one is more specially
charged with the production, the other with the execution.[16]
There is thus a tendency to return to the original state of the
cinema at the time of the silents, when a D. W. Griffith, for
example, was unquestionably—as much as any novelist, to say
nothing of Chaplin—the only one responsible for the films he
made: a situation that gradually changed, especially after the
introduction of sound, under the influence of many causes too
complicated to analyze at this point.

What is important is that the reverse evolution we have
been examining seems true to a profound propensity, more
and more conscious, on the part of the *auteur* of a film to
make it into an *œuvre* in which he will have succeeded in
representing exactly what he has wanted to express. It was
thus quite natural that it should have been Orson Welles—a
man who probably can only tell his own story—who most
clearly and forcefully asserted this tendency. (Gregg Toland,
Citizen Kane's cameraman, wrote that Welles is unequaled in
the efforts he deploys to get exactly what he wants. It is
interesting that the photography of *Citizen Kane* should be
so much like that of *The Magnificent Ambersons,* since different technicians were responsible for the two films.) It seems
as if we are getting closer and closer to the time when the

[16] See Irving Pichel, "La Création doit être l'ouvrage d'un seul,"
Revue du Cinéma, No. 2.

movie, like the novel, will unambiguously and unreservedly be attributable to one author; and it is not impossible to imagine the moment when entire sections of film libraries of the future will proudly be entitled "The Complete Works of" René Clair, Fritz Lang, or Preston Sturges.

2 *The Objective Technique in the American Novel*

In *Voyage to Purilia* Elmer Rice tells the story of a voyage to an ideal country. This strange country of Purilia is nothing other than the materialization of the fantasy worlds of the movies, in which women are separated into carefully delineated castes—the pure young girls, the vamps, the "fallen women"—all differently dressed and immediately identifiable. While you are attentively examining a landscape or a face, it suddenly looms large and takes on enormous proportions: human attention turns everything into a close-up. There are Negroes, but Negroes who eat nothing but chicken or watermelon (which they only really enjoy if they have stolen), who spend their days laughing and singing, and who, if men, earn their living as musicians or Pullman porters and, if women, are former nursemaids of white people who are now giving them small pensions. In this utopia, the social categories of the movies, their vision of the world, and even their modes of perception have taken possession of reality and molded it extensively.

Perhaps we have all become Purilians without knowing it, and we may ask ourselves if the movies' unconscious ascendancy over us has not also, unnoted by the critics, influenced literature. There is nothing strange or unusual about this. We absorb even the most overwhelming influences only indirectly and obscurely, as if we could not bear to become fully aware of too much novelty: an author who has never read a line of Joyce will nevertheless find himself using the interior monologue, whereas fifty years earlier, he might have told his story in the manner of Anatole France or Paul Bourget. Every day, in the streets or in the subway, without being aware of it, we are assaulted by artistic innovations still unfamiliar to us. The poster has educated our visual sensibility by turning the pictorial revolution of impressionism and cubism into common currency. Our ears, trained by jazz and by that movie music no one listens to but everyone hears, are no longer shocked by the dissonances of Stravinsky or Honegger. Long before we ever open *Du Côté de chez Swann (Swann's Way)* or *The Autobiography of Alice B. Toklas,* the newspapers have made us familiar with Proust's *"petite madeleine"*; and reading *Gentlemen Prefer Blondes* has accustomed us to the special idiom of Gertrude Stein. Since the movies have so strongly stirred our sensibilities and wielded such power over the collective consciousness—in which each of us participates, no matter how individualist or withdrawn into himself he thinks himself to be—it would be surprising if they had not exercised any influence on literature.

We all know that today's writers attach great importance to the *technique* of the novel—to all the methods that might serve to make something fresh and subtle of a genre that has become almost classic, that might serve to renew it. One of the surest ways for a young author to capture the attention of both publishers and public is to use an unusual method of narration—to write, for example, an entire novel in the form of interior monologues (as Louis-René Desfôrets did in his first book). But since a new technique rapidly loses its novelty, we are also witnessing the reappearance of novelistic forms that are old-fashioned, yet piquant for that very reason —like the novel written in the form of letters, a style whose masterpieces, Laclos's *Les Liasons dangereuses* and Balzac's *Mémoires de deux jeunes mariées (Letters of Two Brides)* appeared more than a century ago.

A novelist today would feel dishonored if the critics did not make special mention of his "technique" and evoke the names of Faulkner, Hemingway, or Joyce. This is something completely new. At the end of the nineteenth century, the French novel seemed settled in a double tradition: the linear narrative—spare and quasi-autobiographical (at least on the surface)—like *Adolphe* or *Dominique*; and a more recent type—more complex, deliberately objective and impersonal —exemplified by the diverse writings of Flaubert, Maupassant, and Zola that so excited the admiration of foreign writers from Turgenev to Somerset Maugham. In 1944, even this kind of novel is in a state of crisis, experiencing self-doubts and anxiety about its future.

The time is past when Gide could scandalize the literary world by asking: "What is a Balzac compared to a Dostoyevsky? . . . Or, if you prefer, what is a *Princesse de Clèves (The Princess of Cleves)* next to a *Britannicus?*" Today everyone would agree with him, and when Sartre is asked about the French novel, he readily replies with Banville's famous phrase about poetic license: "There is none." Neophytes, recently inspired by Caldwell or Dos Passos, endlessly proclaim that Malraux is nothing compared to Steinbeck, or Bernanos next to Faulkner. This discontent with the state of the French novel is undoubtedly responsible both for the

French writers' perfectly legitimate desire to renew the form by imitating foreign writers and for their ceaseless and growing preoccupation with technical problems, which they have until the past few years given little thought to but which have recently become almost an obsession with some of them. (In the same way the deceptive and somewhat pharisaical security of the France of Poincaré's day abruptly gave way to the dark defeatism of the years 1936–39 and then to the collective breast-beating that followed the June, 1940, armistice.) In literature as in politics, it seems as though the country of measure and moderation can only swing wildly from one extreme to another. But perhaps the French novel does not deserve this excess of either praise or blame—which does not mean that it cannot learn from the American novel or that the desire to create a new narrative technique better adapted to modern sensibilities is not a good thing.

It is possible to explain the current prestige of American literature and the influence it exercises on French writers in terms of either political contingencies or the excellence of the works that have been translated. But there is no doubt another, more basic reason for such a vogue, and I suggest that it is to be found in the cinema's profound modification of our collective sensibility, a modification that has taken place without our even being aware of it. We no longer perceive in the same way as we did fifty years ago; specifically, we have gotten into the habit of *having stories shown to us* instead of hearing them narrated. This must naturally turn storytelling technique upside down.

Because of the extreme traditionalism of French literature, this change has been slow to manifest itself in France, but in America John Dos Passos published his *Manhattan Transfer*—which people spoke of as a "jazz symphony" but which shows more of the influence of cinema than of Negro music—immediately after World War I. This is because the Americans have very little literary tradition. The only tradition that has any sort of reality for them—that puritanical and austere tradition of New England—has from Hawthorne to Henry James remained a local one. Limited to an intellectual caste that chose to orient itself toward the Old World, it does not weigh on the country as a whole as heavily as examples of the last three centuries weigh on France—for instance, Racine's verse on poetry or Voltaire's style on prose. American writers come from more diversified social classes than do French writers. They are not predominantly recruited from among the intellectuals, civil servants, or professors, or from among those whose wealth enables them to dispense with a profession; instead, they have been newsboys, elevator operators, private detectives. They write what they feel, as they feel it and as they see it, without concerning themselves with preestablished literary conventions. Thus, their technique seems more "up-to-date" than that of French writers. In a very precise sense, it reflects more faithfully and expresses more directly the profound upheavals in the consciousness of modern man and in his way of apprehending things.

There is no doubt but that one of the things we love in the American novel is its extreme modernity. This modernity comes not only from its subject but from the very rhythm in which that subject is treated. Dos Passos and Sinclair Lewis please us not only because they paint a picture of a more modern life, further evolved than our own, or because they add the insidious charm of utopia to the classic prestige of exoticism, but because they offer us what may be unique in the world today—a literature in which technique is truly consubstantial with content, with the subject. French writers too often give us an image of modern life as incongruous as a daguerreotype of a skyscraper would be.

Almost all the technical novelties introduced by American

writers (except for the interior monologue,[1] whose historical origin, aesthetic consequences, and metaphysical significance are different) are borrowed by the novel from the film. And this transposition of cinematic methods to literature, which can and probably will be carried even further, is perfectly justified by the basic relationship between the two genres. The result of this transposition has been to make available to the writer a whole new arsenal of extremely efficacious techniques, some of which, of course, had been used long before the invention of the film—though more timidly and less systematically—by Balzac, Stendhal, or the naturalists.

These techniques can be grouped around two major innovations. The first innovation has to do with the method of narration, which becomes absolutely objective, pushed to the point of behaviorism in the name of the very conventions that have been adopted for the presentation of events. These conventions are imposed on the filmmaker by the nature of his art, but they are freely chosen by the modern novelist: events are to be described only from the outside, with neither commentary nor psychological interpretation. The second group of techniques includes the more specifically technical innovations made possible by the extension to the novel of the principle of changing the position of the camera, the discovery of which transformed the cinema by making of it an art. Like the director, the novelist can now permit himself to place his camera wherever he wants, to vary its position continually in such a way as to show us his characters from very far or very near and from unexpected angles, and to let us see a given

[1] As everyone knows, this technique was actually invented by a Frenchman, Edouard Dujardin, and "launched" by Joyce, who drew extraordinary effects from it. The master of the genre is probably another Englishman, Stephen Hudson. But for many of us the "interior monologue" is closely associated with the name of Faulkner, especially with *The Sound and the Fury* and *As I Lay Dying*.

scene from the eyes of first one and then another protagonist —and all this while preserving the continuity necessary to every story, whether printed or filmed. To this major technical innovation can be linked the secondary cinematic techniques used in the novel, such as fade-ins/fade-outs, superimpositions, and crosscuts, many examples of which can be found in American literature.

It is in America that the philosophical school known as "behaviorism" has flourished. Behaviorism is defined by its assumption that the psychological reality of a person or an animal is limited to what can be perceived by a purely external observer (exemplified in its extreme form by the camera lens) and that everything only the subject himself can know, through self-analysis, must be eliminated. In short, psychological reality is to be reduced to a succession of acts, with words or cries having the same weight as gestures or expressions.

Almost every American novelist of the past twenty years, from Hemingway to Caldwell, seems to have unconsciously adopted this behaviorist view of man: they give us not their characters' feelings or thoughts but an objective description of their acts, a court record of their speeches, the minutes of their "conduct" in a given situation. But this behaviorism is for the most part involuntary, thus rarely pure. In Faulkner, for example, interior analysis constantly alternates with descriptions of behavior. This method persists into his most recent works—*The Wild Palms*, for instance—and his abundant use of the interior monologue is sufficient proof of the fact that he does not employ the objective method systematically and rigorously. The master of the genre, the one who has most inflexibly constructed his works according to what might be called the aesthetics of the stenographic record, is Dashiell Hammett, author of *The Maltese Falcon, The Glass*

Key, and *Red Harvest*[2]—books that France unjustly persists in seeing as nothing but simple detective stories. Perhaps this is at least partly so because of the extreme mediocrity of the French translations, which make a book like *Red Harvest* (whose merits are even more subtle than those of Hammett's other two masterpieces) seem banal and practically unreadable.

Hammett's style is generally admirably sparse and austere, thanks precisely to the perfect objectivity with which events are presented. It does not record anything but what we might have seen or heard ourselves if we had been present at the scene—as is the "cameraman" who has been placed there for our benefit. All rhetoric is scrupulously banished from his work, in which the facts are described with the nakedness of a police report. But paradoxically, this simplicity is occasionally obtained only at the expense of clarity: the very rigor with which Hammett limits himself to a behaviorist psychology leads him to complicate his narration and forces him into strange circumlocutions.

For example, because he insists on absolute objectivity, he cannot say "Ned Beaumont felt he was going mad" but must say: "He took the lighter out and looked at it. A cunning gleam came into his one open eye as he looked at the lighter. The gleam was not sane." Since he has chosen to know nothing of his hero's feelings, he cannot write the simple phrase "Despain was afraid" but must write: "Despain stared for a long moment at Ned Beaumont as if horribly fascinated." This results in an occasionally complicated style of expression—Faulkner's obscurity sometimes has a similar origin—which is nevertheless largely redeemed by the ambiguity with which Hammett is able to endow his characters' intentions

---

[2] I am not concerned here with *The Thin Man* or *The Dain Curse*, which are from every point of view quite inferior to the three books cited.

and secret desires, thus surprising us as much as the actors in his dramas by unforeseeable actions and abrupt changes of circumstance.

Because the aesthetic of the stenographic record explains nothing and limits itself to placing the facts before us in all their ambiguity (and all human behavior is ambiguous to the extent that it is not connected to the totality of a personality), it is able to bank on the sure surprise of the reader; it is therefore particularly well suited to the detective story, where it even goes as far as possible toward excusing the author from the more or less unavoidable trickery of camouflaging—to say nothing of suppressing—some of the evidence. Thus, in *The Glass Key*, when Ned Beaumont, after his quarrel with his friend Paul Madwig, goes to Shad O'Rory, the boss of the rival faction, and offers to sell out Paul and his secrets, we are completely fooled and take him for a traitor. When Ned wants to leave, Shad O'Rory, under the pretext of protecting him, retains him by force. From this moment on, Ned refuses to say anything, preferring to let himself be systematically beaten up by Shad's henchmen. We think this is only the stubbornness of the "tough guy" who does not like to give in and who cannot forgive the fact that they have kept him against his will and manhandled him; we do not discover the true reasons for Ned's conduct until much later, when he is in the hospital. After he regains consciousness and his memory returns, he says, "I went there to trap the gent and he outtrapped me."

Until then Beaumont's behavior—and consequently his character—have been completely ambiguous: he seems to have excellent control over himself, but no one is immune to wounded pride, especially tough guys, and we cannot know for sure that he hasn't *really* broken with Madvig when even Madvig himself believes the estrangement between them to be real. Thanks to the strict application of the objective method, Hammett thus succeeded in creating a new type of hero—one whose innermost being was unfathomable and who gave validity to the stereotype popularized by the movies: the strong, silent type who knows how to keep his own counsel and whose decisions always surprise us as much as they do his adversaries; who does not speak because he does not think, thought for him coinciding with action; who no more indulges in interior monologues than he does in conversation, in the social sense of the word; and who nevertheless, thanks to the force with which he asserts himself in the face of events, succeeds in existing for the reader, in being something more than the sum of his acts. He is an ideal character for the detective story and for the movies, but if not described with a kind of genius, he remains a bloodless figure, a nonentity on whom the author tries to confer at least an external existence by means of such superficial mannerisms as an individualistic way of expressing himself, a Herculean strength, a morbid passion for chamber music, cocaine, or French cooking—particularities whose sole intent is to mask his inner nothingness.

Hammett is able to leave his heroes' external appearance and their lives prior to the action in which we see them engaged as vague as he wants. We do not know if they are dark-haired or blond, tall or short, handsome or ugly, but we are not likely to forget Sam Spade of *The Maltese Falcon*, Ned Beaumont of *The Glass Key*, or the narrator of *Red Harvest*—whose name we have most likely never known. No matter how remarkable their actions, they always succeed in being more than their sum, in dominating them; the author has no need to pile on adventitious details, for there is no danger that these heroes will be absorbed into the confusion of events; their personalities will always emerge from the plot, no matter how complex it may be. They exist so strongly that they can dispense with having an inner life.

The use of the objective method in psychology has had the immediate consequence of enlarging the field of study to include animals as well as men. Its application to the novel has had an analogous result—the extreme enrichment of what might be called "the material of the novel," both in terms of the kinds of characters portrayed and the categories of feelings and behavior described. The traditional novel of psychological analysis is only conceivable in a world of leisure and culture, where the characters have the time, the desire, and the intellectual means to observe themselves; *La Princesse de Clèves, Adolphe, À la Recherche du temps perdu*, the novels of Bourget or Radiguet, are good examples. The novel of ideas requires characters who are semiprofessional intellectuals, as was noted by Gide and Huxley, who both tried this kind of writing. Thus, despite the reaction of first naturalism and then populism (both of which broke with the introspective point of view), the French novel at the beginning of the twentieth century was becoming ever more restricted, at least in terms of the choice of subjects and milieus: the major characters of important writers like Proust, Gide, Schlumberger, and Roger Martin du Gard are recruited almost exclusively from the ranks of the upper bourgeoisie. The result is a certain monotony, for the similar sociological determinants of these characters ended by conferring on these characters a certain sameness.

Literature was thus running the risk of becoming somewhat narrow. It is true that one cannot expect to get an adequate idea of a country through its books alone, but it is undeniable that the best French novels of the period between 1914 and 1932 give only a very biased picture of the country, a picture of only the most fortunate of its middle class. The American novel blew a fresh wind into the Republic of Letters. It also had the charm of exoticism—not in the banal sense of something geographically remote but in the more profound sense of social unfamiliarity. It portrays vagabonds, inveterate drunkards, the unemployed; tough guys stripped of all romanticism—simple victims of economic misfortune, caught in the determinism of an inflexible social structure; black people separated from white people by barriers even more insuperable than those of poverty; men who do not know how to read or write and who can barely speak well enough to express their most basic needs. All of them, however, are endowed with an incontestable human reality; all of them, in Christian terms, "have a soul." Because of this, the American novel restores to us, almost unintentionally, a certain idea of *man*, independent of the accidents of class and condition. Truly classic in spirit—classic in the same way as Chaplin's movies, which make people laugh in Shanghai as well as in Romorantin—it is more nearly universal than our eighteenth-century literature because it truly encompasses all races and all classes. It is coextensive with the planet. It demonstrates the principle of a new humanism.

This extension of novelistic material is possible only because of the objective method of description. Steinbeck's stories have the same universality as Chaplin's movies—the universality of mimicry, of a type hardly more developed than in the silent film. Because of its objectivity of vision, the novel can put onstage people of every class, of every intellectual level: characters of the lowest social class, like those in *Tortilla Flat* or *In Dubious Battle*, or retarded people like Lennie in *Of Mice and Men*, or the gallery of idiots like Tommy and Benjy in Faulkner. It is obvious that an author cannot show us beings so lacking self-awareness, so inarticulate, so incapable of expressing themselves, by means of an introspective narrative technique. The idiot Benjy's interior monologue (in *The Sound and the Fury*) constitutes an exceptional technical tour de force, which was only possible because of the extraordinary way in which Faulkner was able to manipulate the language—dislocating it, taking away from it its usual function of discourse and even of meaning, and making the word into an almost verbal equivalent of the image, endowed, like the latter, with its own value and capable of being used as an element in a barrage of vocables rather than as part of the continuity of a rational plot.

Similarly, interior analysis does not really allow for the adequate rendition of violent emotion, drunkenness, delirium, or any state in which consciousness is either nonexistent or reduced to the individual's perception of his constituent elements. In Sartre's "Le Mur" ("The Wall"), Pedro becomes aware of his fear because his pants are wet; the drunk will become conscious of his drunkenness, insofar as he can, when he feels the bench he wants to sit down on treacherously disappear from under him. Dos Passos and Faulkner have given us extraordinary descriptions of drunkenness: that of Stan in *Manhattan Transfer*, just before he sets fire to the house in which he lives; that of Jiggs in *Pylon*. Stan's drunkenness is reduced to the keyhole that turns when he wants to insert the key to open the door, the chair that flies to the window and shatters it, the street that suddenly looms up vertically. In the same way Orson Welles, in *Citizen Kane*, shows his hero's anger by photographing the piles of furniture he has just broken up, while his inner solitude, the emptiness created around him by his pride, are concretized by the large funereal rooms of the huge and deserted castle he has built for himself. Here it is not even the behavior of human beings that is revealing, but that of things: describing this behavior shows us more than would any analysis of a perhaps non-existent state of awareness, especially since in any case the content of that awareness is limited to the perception of such behavior.

Even more important than this enrichment of novelistic material are the aesthetic results of strict objectivity in the narration. Every interpretation of, every commentary on, a naked fact tends to weaken the shock to our sensibility. Stendhal and Balzac were well aware of this; they allowed events to bear down on us—like the train, in those three-dimensional movies, that suddenly fills both the screen and our consciousness. Without a word of explanation, Stendhal gives us Julien's pistol shot, Mathilde's rearranged hair the morning after her night of love, Clélia's voice suddenly saying, "Come here, my heart's beloved"; and this restrained presentation is considerably more eloquent than anything he might have achieved by analyzing the feelings of Julien, Mathilde, or Clélia to arrive at the perhaps unknowable, possibly non-existent psychological reality that is behind and the cause of his characters' behavior. In the same way, in *La Femmé abandonée (A Forsaken Lady)*, Balzac throws M. de Neuil's suicide at us thus:

> An hour later, when the Caprice had come to an end, and the husband and wife sat in silence on opposite sides of the hearth, the man came back from Valleroy and gave his master his own letter, unopened.
> M. de Neuil went into a small room beyond the drawing room, where he had left his rifle on returning from hunting, and shot himself.[3]

We could not be less prepared for this suicide of a man who has seemed to us egotistical, superficial, and certainly unworthy of the love of Madame Blauseant. It is exactly this element of surprise that Balzac counts on, just as Hammett does when he relates some unexpected behavior on the part of Sam Spade or Ned Beaumont. And Balzac gives us no more explanation than Stendhal, even after we have had time to

[3] Honoré de Balzac, *Balzac's Works*, New York, Hearst's International Library, Vol. 6, p. 43.—Tr.

take in the shock; on the contrary, he says, "There's nothing to be surprised about, you might have expected it." The twenty-odd lines that follow the story's brutal denouement are sententious rather than analytic—the commentary of a moralist, not a psychologist. They also have an aesthetic function, which is more to calm us than to enlighten us. Like Racine's twenty-odd stanzas that follow the death of Phèdre and lead the play to the final curtain, they are meant to prepare the reader for a return to daily life, to serve as a transition to reality, to allow the artistic emotion to subside gently after having reached its highest point. Similarly, in *La Duchesse de Langeais (The Duchess of Langeais)* we are given no explanation for the heroine's extraordinary about-face: just as Montriveau is about to brand her, she suddenly realizes that she loves him madly. The author leaves us free to make what we will of this. His job is to place the facts before us, not to help us understand them.

The novel thus appears to be much less an art of language than we might a priori have expected it to be. Its aim is to *show* rather than to *say*, and it is therefore related to the cinema even when it is not in the least influenced by it. The great lesson the American novel learned from the movies—that the less one says the better, that the most striking artistic effects are those born of the juxtaposition of two images, without any commentary, and that the novel, no more than any other art, should not say too much—was very well understood by Hemingway, Faulkner, and Steinbeck. But Stendhal, Balzac, and the naturalists had anticipated it: long before the twentieth century, they had already invented the journalistic novel. At the end of *Pylon* there is an incident meant to communicate the very Faulknerian notion of the tragic irony of fate: the comrades of a dead aviator have bled themselves dry to get together a little money for his widow and child; not daring to offer it to her directly, they hide it in a little toy airplane intended for the child, who is going to live with his grandparents. The grandfather finds the money, believes it to have been put there by his daughter-in-law—whom he considers a tramp—in an attempt to hide her ill-gotten gains from her husband, and throws the money into the fire. Maupassant had already used the same kind of incident, however, presented without any kind of commentary, in "La Ficelle" ("A Piece of String"), "La Parure" ("The Necklace"), and "Le Petit Fût" ("The Little Cask") to express the same sense of the tragic futility of human effort. Horror is another strong feeling that could only be weakened by commentary. Faulkner no more has to insist, at the end of *Sanctuary*, on the atrocious fate that befalls Joe Goodwin, burned alive by the mob for a crime he did not commit, than Maupassant had to emphasize the terror inherent in "La Peur" ("Fear"), "L' Auberge" ("The Inn"), or "Le Horla" ("The Horla").

Because of this aesthetic imperative of discretion and taciturnity, one might even say that the novel, like the cinema, is essentially an art of ellipsis. We have seen the striking effects that are obtained when emotionally charged events are presented to us without commentary, in all their nakedness. When they are even more sensational, the novelist, like the filmmaker, would do best not to speak of them at all, but to suggest them indirectly. This was the method generally used in Pierre Benoit's first novels (*Mademoiselle de la Ferté, L'Atalantide, Alberte,* and *Axelle*): to conceal the essential fact from the reader in order to oblige him to reconstruct it, little by little, by conjectures and make it gradually emerge from the matrix of mystery in which it was hidden.

In the same way, Faulkner does not show us the central facts on which everything in *Sanctuary* depends: Temple's sexual violation with the corncob and, concomitantly, Tommy's murder. The reason for this is analogous to that which often makes the cinema elliptical—the too-shocking nature of the event. This conjuring away of the essential is almost classic in Faulkner: in *Light in August* it is only gradually that we become aware of Christmas's crime and of his black blood, and in *The Sound and the Fury* the method is carried to its ultimate conclusion, since by virtue of the technique that has been chosen, *nothing* can be told us directly—we are only given the refraction of events in the consciousness of the characters, and to such an extent that we are not explicitly told about Benjy's castration until past the middle of the book and then only through Jason's interior monologue.

It is obvious that the novel is led to ellipsis for the same reason as is the cinema: an obligation to honesty that obliges the storyteller to show only those facts his camera might have been able to see without cheating—or, in other words, a respect for the conventions that define his art. The elliptical nature of that art thus proceeds from a kind of nonsubjective impressionism; it results from a convention analogous to that which forbids the novelist all recourse to interior analysis. Faulkner, as well as modern American novelists in general, has chosen never to show us a scene by describing it in abstract terms and from all points of view (for example, if it were a case of Mary Stuart's execution, from the different points of view of Mary, the executioner, Elizabeth, and the spectators). In other words, instead of presenting an event in a manner such as no one except possibly God himself could ever have seen, these novelists show it only as any given spectator might have seen it (the camera naturally being able to move rapidly from one point of view to another, but not being able to adopt every point of view simultaneously). They eliminate from the narrative the things no consciousness could be aware of, the things no lens could have recorded.

In the novel as in the film, a certain kind of ellipsis thus appears as the direct consequence of the objectivity— voluntary in the writer, obligatory in the filmmaker—that forbids the artist to show the public anything that could not have been seen by a recording apparatus. But the use of a rhetoric often has unforseen consequences. As we shall see, this technique, which seems on the surface to be so purely formal, not only permits certain aesthetic effects but occasionally serves to cloak a metaphysical meaning as well.

3 *Ellipsis in the Movies and in the Novel*

By the very nature of its technique, the cinema was destined to be an art of ellipsis. The myths surrounding its birth would have it that the discovery of its nature (like the even more important discovery of the mobility of the camera equipment) was due at least partly to chance. When Chaplin was making *A Woman of Paris*, which takes place in France, he did not have available to him French railway cars, which are quite different from American railway cars. He therefore decided to film the departure of the train by showing us not the slowly moving cars but only the gradually accelerating passage of lights and shadows on the face of Edna Purviance, the abandoned young lady left standing on the station platform. The scene had an almost unbearable emotional power. The movies had discovered the infinite power of suggestion.

This lesson was understood by the novel in its turn. Just as the arrival and departure of the train in *A Woman of Paris* are reduced to reflections on a face, so in Faulkner is Benjy's castration known mainly by its refraction through the consciousness of others. But these teachings could be applied even more systematically. The director gives the writer the example of audacity; he also shows him how audacity can serve his purpose. The novelist can learn from him the value of significant details: thanks to the movies, he can learn that to represent a crime it is sufficient to show the assassin's finger on the trigger of the revolver, an open mouth about to scream, a woman's horrified face in the crowd—and that one can do without the detonation, the sight of the falling body, the arrival of the police.

We find it surprising that the authors of *La Vida es Sueño, Volpone,* or *Les Fourberies de Scapin* should have thought it necessary to show us the characters first plotting their nefarious schemes and then carrying them out in front of our eyes. This duplication seems to us useless, sometimes even boring. Art in our time undoubtedly depends more on the element of surprise than it did in the time of the Elizabethans or the Classicists, but the quick narrative rhythm of the films is probably also responsible for our impatience with redundancies. French novelists, weighed down with the tradition of their art, often give us the same impression of old-fashioned heaviness, and we want to write in the margins of their books the traditional American annotation: "Make it a little slicker!"[1] Too timid, they are always afraid that the reader will not understand, so they do his work for him. The filmmaker is more audacious (as surprising as this may be in what passes for a popular art) and has confidence in the spectator. His technique obliges him to be sparing with explanations, so he allows the spectator to manage as best he can with the images he presents to him.

Chemistry would perhaps never have been born if our scales had from the very beginning been extremely sensitive.

[1] In English in the original text.—Tr.

In the same way, we should probably be grateful that the slowness of technical progress obliged the cinema to go through a long period of silence. It is true that at first we paid for the excitement of sound with a period of filmed theater, but dialogue now seems to have become in good movies what it should never have stopped being: the brilliant finishing touch that brings a sequence to perfection—as in *Le Jour se lève* or *Le Crime de M. Lange*, in which Jacques Prévert's texts provide the setting for Carné's or Renoir's images. Its function in the novel, an art of language, will naturally be different. But the example of the movies may preserve the novelist—an overconscientious pedagogue—from the temptation that threatens every man as soon as he speaks: didacticism. It will show him the value of condensation and make him dream of an art in which words will have acquired the poignancy of images and will be able to communicate the same ephemeral anguish, the same implacable and discrete emotion. This is a vain and exaggerated ambition, but one that is salutary by virtue of its very exaggeration.

This dream largely explains Faulkner's obscurity. In the dark tangle of *Sanctuary*, as in the more peaceful though still lightning-streaked scenes of *Light in August*, he wanted to achieve—without forcing himself to the meticulous preparations of a Balzac—the ecstatic consummation of an all-but-unbearable emotion in which language, though it has created it, almost disappears. Just as a passionate actress "burns up the boards," so Faulkner, at the climactic point of his stories, burns his words; he sacrifices them to this myth of a novelistic art that will no longer *explain* anything but which will be beyond language—an art that will restore to us, without recourse to pointless chatter, the brief incandescence of the supreme moments of existence. Why should we be surprised that he does not always have that discursive clarity to which French novelists have accustomed us? His art is the dream of a speech that would no longer speak, but simply *be*. In his impatience to have his vision flash before us, he gets entangled in words, he stammers phrases of apparent incoherence—like a man who has too much to say and too little time to say it in.

Whether or not this dream has come to the novelist through conscious meditation about the cinema is unimportant. The limits of his art are incessantly and sharply brought to his attention by the example of this kindred art. At the end of *Angels with Dirty Faces* one image by Michael Curtiz is sufficient to inform the spectator of the resolution of a psychological conflict: when the gangster walks toward the electric chair, we see his knees buckle, and we know he is going to die as a coward, or rather, in the context of the movie, as a hero, because he feigns a terror he does not at all feel so that this coward's death will destroy his prestige in the eyes of the young boys. A critic needs five lines to explain the significance of something the image gives us instantaneously.

Novelists like Hammett and Caldwell have systematically tried to imbue their art with this cinematic restraint and objectivity. It is even possible that the movies, generally considered an instrument that dulls perception, may actually reeducate the perception and intelligence of the spectator by accustoming him to understand things without long explanations. It is true that the comprehension he develops is beyond language and cannot easily be expressed in words, but that is exactly why the cinema constitutes a healthy reaction against our civilization, which is so overstuffed with words. In any case, it is in no way a passive pleasure or a predigested nourishment for our aesthetic sensibility or our spirit. The movies train the public to subtlety, the novelist to restraint. They teach the latter that dialogue should be descriptive or, if you prefer, narrative, but never explanatory. In other words, dialogue must serve, just as images do, to show the actions, behavior, or attitudes of the characters, not to communicate the author's hints about their secret intentions. This is the natural function of dialogue in Hammett's *Maltese Falcon* and *Glass Key*, where the characters' comments are hardly less opaque or enigmatic than their actions, or in Steinbeck's *In Dubious Battle*, where it is integrated with the action and is merely one element among others.

Because of the novelist's desire for circumspection, there is the risk that his carefully thought-out effects will remain unperceived. Hammett's greatness is too often unrecognized because he has not drawn the reader's attention to the significance of his work. Some of the filmmaker's most subtle effects are also never noticed by the average spectator, even when he is forewarned about them. How many people have noticed, during the great explanation scene between Jules Berry and Jean Gabin in *Le Jour se lève*, the drop of water that slowly slides down the siphon, both suggesting and taking the place of the tear about to fall from the eyes of Jules Berry, moved by the emotional force of his own lies? In *Queen Christina*, how many spectators are aware of the heroine's strange mores as suggested by the perhaps excessive tact displayed by Rouben Mamoulian, caught between censorship requirements and his desire to evoke everything? Does this mean that the director's subtlety is useless?

Actually, here too the cinema offers the language arts a salutary example of the spirit of sacrifice. By its very nature, literature supports the two-thousand-year-old prejudice of Western civilization in favor of clarity. This is because in order for something to *be* in literature, it has to be expressed. Because nothing that is not clearly perceived is effective, we are led to belittle the value of indirect suggestion and to consider as unimportant those aesthetic effects that take place outside the center of interest and are more or less unperceived by intelligence. Literature normally tends toward pure prose—

that is, toward a form of expression perfectly identical with itself, equally devoid of both mystery and implications, in which there is nothing beyond what is said and immediately understood.

Fortunately, during the course of history several arts have come to the rescue and protected literature from itself, preserving in it some areas of silence and safeguarding the rights of poetry. At the end of the nineteenth century such was the function of music in relation to the symbolist movement. Today this may be the role of the movies. Valéry, thinking of Wagner, dreamed of a literature that would, like the latter's orchestration, know how to create "in the shadow of the auditory sense, in the distant and defenseless regions of the sensitive soul, the far-off events, the presentiments, the questions, the enigmas, the undefinable stirrings . . ."[2] He wanted an art that would, like music, know how to speak to the unconscious. But the cinema, no less than music, acts directly on the "sensitive soul": like music, it speaks to the senses without having to pass through the intermediary of understanding; it is, in the etymological sense of the word, *aesthetic* rather than intellectual. And that is why it is able to avoid the error that constantly threatens the language arts—the error of reducing human consciousness to only its most rational part and speaking to that part alone.

In the movies we do not have to be fully conscious of something in order for it to *be*. In *Pay Day*, Charlie Chaplin, drunk, goes into a delicatessen that he mistakes for a trolley car. He hangs onto a salami just as naturally as a real passenger hangs onto the car straps, and he distractedly tries to pay his fare to the shopkeeper who wants to make him leave. This scene produces the same effect on the illiterate coolie in Shanghai as on the blasé intellectual of Montparnasse or

[2] "Le Retour de Hollande," in *Variété II*.

Greenwich Village. It brings to these diverse consciousnesses the same more or less clearly perceived cluster of layered meanings—from the most concrete, the most elementary, which one is obliged to give to the scene in order to be able to describe it in words ("Charlie mistakes the delicatessen for a trolley"), to the most abstract, the most philosophical, which would have to be translated by something like "Charlie imitates the behavior of men inappropriately, carrying out in one situation acts suitable to another" and would be able to serve as illustrations of the Bergsonian theory of comedy like "something mechanical superimposed on something living." The superiority of visual to intellectual art comes from the fact that a scene's aesthetic power is more or less independent of the clarity with which these layered meanings are perceived: the coolie will laugh not one whit less than the intellectual. Chaplin's longtime mistrust of sound is quite understandable: it is silence that bestows on his art, as on Harpo Marx's, its special position; it is his mutism that makes him truly international. Because his language is not made up of words, because it is apprehended rather than understood, it can affect men of all ages, of all classes, of all nations, and—especially—of all intellectual levels.

Chaplin's art is the ultimate expression of cinema. All literature could learn from cinema the lesson John Dos Passos learned from it: to use the marginal areas of the reader's consciousness without fearing that every detail not clearly perceived by the reader is lost, without dismissing as unimportant those meanings that remain implicit. In his *U.S.A.* trilogy, Dos Passos frames his narrative with documentary or poetic fragments that seem to have no direct bearing on the story: the Newsreels, the lyrical biographies of famous people, the interior monologues of anonymous people we know nothing about and who are not part of the story. The reader, who wants to know "what happens next" and who is disturbed by the bizarre nature of these fragments, reads them rapidly, with only half an eye. Only after a second or third reading will he get a dim idea of their significance or their interest, just as it is only after a second or third viewing of *Le Jour se lève* that the drop of water on the siphon will be noticed.

Since for most spectators and readers there will be no second or third time, does this mean that all the work of the director and the novelist has been for nothing? Certainly not, for no matter how inattentive or rapid the first perception may have been, a detail that has not consciously registered as a separate impression has nonetheless acted as a fragment of a whole. The first time I listened to *Boris Godunov*, I probably did not notice that the theme of Pimen or of the faithful Witness reappeared at a particular moment: if I did notice it, it was certainly not in the same way that I hear the melody "Elle avait une jambe de bois . . . " in *Petrouchka*. Yet Mussorgsky's intent is no more lost than is Stravinsky's.

The modern work that has best understood this double lesson of music and film is unquestionably Joyce's *Ulysses*, and Joyce's example, as much as that of the movies, may have encouraged Dos Passos in his polyphonic ambitions. Historically, Joyce's aim was undoubtedly to confer on the novel the same powers over the unconscious as music has, but that did not prevent his attempts from converging at several points with those of the filmmakers: it is surely not by pure chance that the aesthetic of *Finnegans Wake* so evokes, in certain places, that of the animated cartoon. It is thus not surprising that the undeniable influence of Joyce on Dos Passos should combine with the influence of cinematic technique to enlarge the traditional ambition of the novel and to reintroduce into literature some purely *aesthetic* elements, the functions of which are neither discursive nor narrative.

The more our attention is concentrated on the sense of the words pronounced by a voice, the less sensitive we are to

the harmonious timbre of the voice; in the same way, in language arts, the more dry and prosaic the text, the poorer it is
in elements capable of being apprehended by the unconscious
alone. The systematic imitation of the movies could bring to
the narrative the same multidimensional depth given a poem
by rhythm, rhyme, and assonance, or the multiple and subjective association of images called into being by the juxtaposition of vocables. The poetic counterpoint that even the most
austere novelist cannot keep himself from surrounding his
work with should be silent, just as the filmmaker's is—or, at
least, since it can hardly be made with anything other than
words, it should be resolutely nondiscursive, for it is to the
"sensitive soul" that it is addressing itself. From the movies,
literature in our generation is relearning the profound lesson
that its nature often betrays: that of being a total art addressing itself to man as a whole—not only to the most intellectual,
the most lucid, and yet the most limited part of his being.

We have come a long way from the naïve conception of
ellipsis as a simple technical procedure that allows one to tell a
story more elegantly or to treat with restraint scabrous themes
it would otherwise be impossible to raise to the dignity of art.
Its significance, however, is not limited to the aesthetic effects it permits or to the larger conception of art it suggests.
Its essential importance is metaphysical, as is that of the objective method of narration from which it directly derives.

Two novels—one American, the other French—show in
an unexpected way this desire for absolute objectivity now
common to a whole current of literature. In *U.S.A.*, Dos Passos tells his characters' stories in the third person, but the
point of view is only superficially an external one. The story
would be exactly the same if the character said "I," for we
are told not only about his behavior but about his emotions,
his preoccupations, his psychological reactions; we are told

things about him that only he can know. The use of the third person is nevertheless justified: John Dos Passos's characters think of themselves in the same terms as would be used by others who perceive them; their "inner life" flows along spontaneously in a world of preconceived notions, ready-made expressions. True, their lives are described as they themselves might describe them, but as told to a third person, with the same clichés they would use in conversation and without the least effort to come any closer to an individual psychological reality, an ineffable self-knowledge—almost certainly nonexistent in them. They do not have an "inner self"; there is nothing personal in them that might be reached by analysis; their consciousness is nothing more than a web of conventional opinions received from the social group they belong to, and regularly translated into the vocabulary of that group.

This means that the novelist, in his attempt to re-create the individual quality of these consciousnesses, does not have the right to use the interior monologue or any other method of direct presentation, for that would be to mask the characters' profound emptiness, lend them an appearance of individuality, make us believe that they truly have a psychological depth, a third dimension. The narrative has to be "in the third person" in every sense of the phrase, because even when they are alone with themselves Dos Passos's characters are always speaking to an imaginary "third person." Our uneasiness before this ambiguous method of presentation, neither objective (since we are introduced, so to speak, to the "behind-the-scenes" personality of the character instead of being limited to seeing only his facade, as in Hammett) nor subjective (since he is spoken of as if he were not there, in extremely conventional language), is deliberate: it enables us to apprehend, as if by chance, just how psychologically adulterated these people are. Because of their lack of solidity, their absolute emptiness, this sense of adulteration is the impression we would get if we were to find ourselves face to face with them. Dos Passos's highly individual technique is thus the exact opposite of an artistic trick: it is the only way in which he can communicate his completely personal vision of humanity. Like every perfect technique, it ceases to be a technique and becomes the direct expression of an original conception of man and the world.

One could say that the most important thing in Dos Passos's novels is what is not said. Chaplin noted that the two innovations of *A Woman of Paris* were, first, to show the arrival and departure of a train without showing the train and, second, to make no attempt either to show or to explain the gap of a year in the life of a woman. We know that what Proust most admired in *L'Éducation sentimentale* was the "blank" that followed the death of Sénécal, in which fifteen years of Frédéric's life were disposed of in a cinematic rhythm: "He traveled. He knew the melancholy of steamboats, the cold awakenings under the tent, the numbing effect of scenery and ruins, the bitterness of interrupted friendship." The importance of this "blank" is the same as that of the silence in *A Woman of Paris:* it gives us the sensation of "dead time," of passing years that bring nothing new, of years during which, on the contrary, there is nothing but the deterioration of the self. We leave Edna Purviance vainly awaiting her fiancé on a station platform; we next see her as the mistress of a rich man. What is there to say about her development during the year that separates the two situations, since this development has nothing either positive or constructive about it—since during this time the heroine has done nothing but wear herself out and disintegrate? Only ellipsis, silence, the refusal to say anything, can adequately express this loss of reality, this absence of self, this abdication from existence.

In *Manhattan Transfer* Dos Passos uses an analogous technique. We leave the heroine, Ellen, on a doorstep, announcing to Jimmy Herf (who has long been in love with her) that she is expecting a baby and that Stan, her lover who has just been burned alive, is the father. We pick her up on a boat leaving for France, married to Jimmy and pregnant with his baby. In the interval, only one brief scene has given us any information, and we are not even sure that the young woman in the scene is Ellen: a young woman goes to a doctor for an abortion and explains that she has to have it because of her career. What else could the novelist tell us, what kind of explanations could he give us, to illuminate Ellen's behavior? Even an interior monologue would only give us her intellectual reasons or rationalizations, and those we can easily guess, since they are determined by her situation (worry about her career, need for protection, the necessity for social respectability both for herself and for her baby), of which we are already aware. A psychological analysis would be superfluous because it would not enable us to reach Ellen's deep reality, which most likely does not exist. Ellipsis thus seems to be the only technique adequate to the experience of nothingness— the only one capable of expressing it in literature.

In *L'Étranger* (*The Stranger*) Camus systematically uses ellipsis to express a particular form of nonbeing—the absurd. His problem is to present us with events that have carefully been sifted, filtered, in such a way as to remove from them all meanings not appropriate to his purpose. Mersault, his hero, kills an Arab on the beach:

> The trigger gave, and the smooth underbelly of the butt jogged my palm. And so, with that crisp, whipcrack sound, it all began. . . . But I fired four shots more into the inert body, on which they left no visible trace. And each successive shot was another loud, fateful rap on the door of my undoing.[3]

[3] Albert Camus, *The Stranger*, trans. by Gilbert Stuart, New York, Random House, 1946, p. 76.—Tr.

There is nothing sensational in this description of a murder: every horrible detail has been removed as nonessential. There is no analysis of the murderer's mind, either; he is absent from himself, at this moment more than ever. The only significance of the act that the filter has allowed to pass through is its inevitability: in an absurd universe the only function of human acts is to form a destiny. This is why during the second part of the story, during the trial, the most casual, the most insignificant acts of the first part—Mersault drinking coffee, going to the movies, swimming with his girlfriend—seem suddenly imbued with a sinister meaning. They lead to the murder of the Arab, and the jurors can only see in them the sign of a perverted nature. Mersault is condemned as much for not having cried at his mother's funeral as for having killed a man. One can understand why the only subjective impression the author has allowed to figure in his story of a murder should be, "And each successive shot was another loud, fateful rap on the door of my undoing."

Everywhere else in the novel Camus's artificial filtering consists of the presentation of a character who says "I" while telling us only what a third person might know of him. He does not say "I felt like shooting the Arab" (and actually he is not conscious of feeling anything like that), but "The trigger gave. . . . I fired four shots more . . . "; not "I wanted Maria," but "She had a pretty dress with red and white stripes and leather sandals." This is exactly the opposite of Dos Passos's method. What is subjective in the latter is objective in the former, and vice versa, yet the method of narration achieves the same ambiguity in *L'Étranger* as in *U.S.A.* It provokes the same uneasiness, through which the author is able to communicate his desolate vision of an absurd universe, peopled by consciousnesses without solidity, where emotions, desires, and wishes find momentary resting places without our ever being able to understand the precise laws governing their appearance or disappearance. Mersault is the *container* of his feelings and his intentions; he does not produce them. He knows no more of their origins or their workings than any spectator of his actions. One might say that his life projects itself on a screen as it unfolds and that he observes it from without. He does not succeed in finding within himself the feelings or psychological reactions he looks for (sadness during the death of his mother, love for Maria, regret for the murder of the Arab) but sees only what others can see—his acts. He thus appears as a "stranger" to himself: he sees himself as others see him, from the same vantage point as they do. The technical paradox of Camus's narration is to be falsely introspective, as that of Dos Passos was falsely objective.

Of course, Camus was not the first to present us with characters who, when speaking of themselves, limit themselves to reporting their acts, their behavior, and who seem to be ignorant of what is going on in their minds. In two of James M. Cain's novels—*The Postman Always Rings Twice* and *Serenade*—the character says "I," as does the narrator of *Red Harvest*, who gives us as impartial a stenographic record of his actions as possible. But the technique remains a simple method of exposition, one it would not have been inconceivable to replace by another: the effect Hammett obtains in *Red Harvest* is not appreciably different from that of *The Maltese Falcon*, where the story unfolds in the third person, as is normal in an objective narrative.

This superficial resemblance between Camus's technique and that of some American novelists explains one of the descriptions of *L'Étranger* as "Kafka written by Hemingway." It was said simply because Hemingway is one of the best-known authors regularly using this method. But the profound significance of the technique is absolutely different. What is new in *L'Étranger* is its use of the subtle dissonance between an objective description of events and a first-person narration—

which is usually, especially in the French tradition, introspective—to communicate a very personal conception of man and
the world. Camus wants us to see his character's inner nothingness—and, beyond this, our own nothingness, the nothingness of we who are his brothers. Mersault is man denuded of
all the ready-made coverings with which society clothes the
normal emptiness of his being; he roughly corresponds to what
a Dos Passos character would be if he were deprived of all
the clichés and conventional feelings that fill his consciousness. Faced with the death of his mother, he does not find
within himself the unhappiness he is supposed to feel; his
emotion is reduced to a few acts that do not make much sense
—spending the night next to the body and following the
funeral cortege the next day. He horrifies the society whose
hypocrisy he rejects. He scandalizes the critics just as, in the
novel, he infuriates the judges and jurors. He is Voltaire's
Huron in *L'Ingénu*, Huxley's Savage in *Brave New World*—a
man whose very existence strikingly shows up the vanity of
society's efforts to mask from us the nothingness we are.

This brings us to the profound truth revealed to us by
the very nature of the objective technique: inner life does
not exist; the psychological level does not reveal any reality;
consciousness is not important. All this becomes obvious if one
restricts oneself to describing a human life from the outside,
deleting all subjective elements. This truth, so distressing to
our pride, can already be glimpsed in *L'Éducation sentimentale*, and it blazes out from Maupassant's "Une Vie" ("A
Life"). Man always has less of an inner life than he thinks,
and especially if his idea of an inner life is based on faith in
traditional introspection. He is little more than a "republic of
reflexes." Such is the cheerless lesson that can be learned from
naturalism.

But it is not necessary to stop there. To avoid despair,
one can add that man's only reality is to be found in his

spiritual life, which is ethical or metaphysical in nature, not psychological. Trapped between the level of acts and the level of values, the level of psychology in its real sense—that which one would attain by introspection—is not autonomous. When the Duchess of Langeais flirts with Montriveau, Balzac does not analyze her feelings: he barely gives us even a portion of what she says. The rest is left to our imagination—or to Giraudoux's. This is because a description of what the duchess says is no more important than a description of what she feels. Neither description would at all enlighten us about what she does, which is completely reducible to physiological and social determinants. During this period of her life, the Duchess has no inner being; like Edna Purviance in *A Woman of Paris*, like Ellen in *Manhattan Transfer*, she is nothing—at least nothing that can be understood by introspection. Comte's criticisms of psychology are completely justified here.

Dos Passos's characters would also constitute a striking illustration. A profound truth about modern man emerges from *U.S.A.*—that he can be reduced to the triple determinism of hunger, sexuality, and social class: Pavlov, Freud, and Marx. Language and consciousness are superimposed: the real truth about Eleanor Stoddard or Charley Anderson is not to be found in what they say or in what they think about themselves. The method borders on satire at every moment, but it is a metaphysical satire rather than a social one, a revolt against the essence of the human condition rather than against this or that form of society. It is Man, or Being, not Capitalism or American society, that is taken to task in the novels of Hammett or Camus—and even in those of Dos Passos, despite their elements of social protest.

It is certainly not an accident that the important novels of the recent past, be they French or American, all suggest the same conclusion, which is also that of Marxism and psychoanalysis: the nonexistence of the psychological, the futility and even the fraudulence of introspection. In Platonic or Cartesian language, the psychological seems like a mixture, analogous—in the hierarchy of the elements—to mud, the vile mélange of earth and water that dares not be either purely solid or purely liquid. The traditional novel of introspection gives us this mud, dried by analysis and crumbling into dust before our eyes. It gives us an ignoble counterfeit of the inner life, our personal mythology, the ersatz of what authentic moral aspirations would be. As soon as man contemplates himself, he cannot help but dramatize himself; sometimes, if he has genius, he gives birth to an interesting fable—like one a talented mythomaniac might create, but lacking the least bit of truth. The novel of analysis automatically tends to give him too proud an idea of himself, to mask from him his true incoherence, to persuade him of his false dignity as a "thinking reed." The novel of objective technique proposes a completely different conception of man, and thus it is scandalous.

The lighthearted equivalent of this conception can be found in the charming "absurd" (or, if you prefer, "screwball") American comedies of the thirties; they also often shock the public even while amusing it. By showing us these nondimensional characters, systematically inconsistent, the directors of *Bringing Up Baby, My Man Godfrey, Mr. and Mrs. Smith, The Lady and the Tramp*, and many others are only following to its logical conclusion one of the aesthetic directions open to the cinema by virtue of its technique: since showing characters only from the outside gives an impression of incoherence and superficiality, one can take maximum advantage of this incoherence and superficiality and make it the aesthetic aim of the work. Because of the movie's lively rhythm and deliberate lack of seriousness, the absurdity is gay, while in the novel it is almost always despairing. The reactions of the film critic to this kind of comedy—at least when the zaniness is not overlaid by a pretense of social criticism, as in the films of Capra—are of the same order as the reactions of "sensible" critics to *L'Étranger*. The only difference is that the former do not have to take the movie seriously because of the deliberate lightness of the genre, and they can thus look down on it rather than get angry about it.

These analyses show how polymorphous is the role of ellipsis, this new rhetoric common to both the movies and the contemporary novel. Initially an immediate consequence of the hyperobjective method of narration, it quickly acquired a value and significance of its own as a method fertile in aesthetic effects and, in addition, pregnant with an implicit metaphysic. It ended by serving as a kind of counterweight to the desired objectivity from which it had originally sprung. Thanks to ellipsis, the will of the author—indispensable for true aesthetic creation—has been reintroduced into the work of art. Ellipsis—understood in the broadest sense as a choice of elements, some (the images of film) registered mechanically, others (the novelistic description of the characters' behavior) reproducing reality as faithfully and impartially as possible—allows the presentation of raw material ordered in terms of a desired specific artistic effect, that is, of meaning. It consequently permits the reintroduction of the author's subjectivity and will, whether that *auteur* be director or writer. By means of this will, art accentuates and invigorates the paradox that is the very principle of perception: vision is the arbitrary act of will par excellence, that by which we choose to see right-side up the objects which in reality are painted upside down on our retinas. The right to an arbitrary vision of the world is the most sacred, the most inalienable right of man. Art only proclaims out loud this too-often-forgotten right.

To this will that enters into the selection of elements obtained by methods as objective as possible, one can superimpose another, perfectly compatible with the objectivity and even the mechanical character of the recording instrument: the will that consists of varying either the distance between the object and the recording mechanism or the angle of view in such a way as to obtain elements that remain objective yet sustain different relations to reality. In movies the operation by which a scene is arranged into a sequence of shots—that is, of variable camera positions—is called cutting. We shall see that the succession of different kinds of shots is a method no more necessarily limited to movies than are ellipsis or the objective technique, and that one can as well speak of "cutting" in the contemporary novel (especially in the American novel, which seems to have made almost systematic use of it) as in the movies.

4 Cutting in the Movies and in the Novel

According to Malraux,[1] the cinema became an art the day it was accidentally discovered that the camera, being independent of the represented scene, could be made mobile in relation to that scene. Legend has it that this major transformation was due to chance. D. W. Griffith was supposed to have been so moved by the beautiful face of an actress playing a role in one of his movies that he rephotographed the face, this time from nearby, and later interpolated the shot into the sequence of images. The close-up was born.

Cinema stopped being a somewhat improved kind of photography, broadened in scope by movement, stopped being a simple way of *representing* things by reproducing them mechanically, and became an art, capable of *expressing* something. It could no longer be content with merely filming theater scenes; these scenes, either before or after they were filmed, would have to be redistributed to achieve a desired effect. This redistribution, otherwise known as cutting, is made possible by the mobility of the camera.

[1] In his "Esquisse d'une psychologie du cinéma," in *Verve*.

It is remarkable that the novel should have taken three centuries to claim the same liberty in "shooting" images. It could easily have done so at any time, since it did not even require, as did the cinema, a physical act such as the actual displacement of the recording apparatus, which though real for the moviemaker is purely imaginary for the novelist. The truth is that the novel was so content with being a linear narrative—most often, as in *Gil Blas* or *Adolphe*, told in the voice of the main character—that it felt no need for a new technique. Even when it is not the main character who says "I," the imaginary camera of the novelist is in fact installed in the consciousness of the hero—as in *Le Rouge et le noir* (*The Red and the Black*), for example, where the narrative's perspective is always that of Julien Sorel.

As long as a novel's interest remains centered on the experiences of an individual, it has no use for a constantly changing point of view on the events being related: with the reader invited to identify with the hero, the recording apparatus, which is the consciousness of that hero, remains fixed. It was only toward the end of the nineteenth century, when writers wanted to go beyond the individual and design a fresco of a family, or even of an epoch, that they had to create a more flexible technique. The introduction into the novel of changes in perspective analogous to those of the cinema was made necessary by the vast inner transformation of the novel, a transformation that began with Zola and continues today, especially in the United States. There has been a transition from the novel-as-story-of-an-individual to the novel-as-story-of-a-collectivity—the evolution of the narrative toward an impersonal art.

It is not by accident that the major writers who find themselves constantly passing from the close-up to the long shot—Proust, Gide, Malraux, Dos Passos, Steinbeck—are precisely those who want their books to give us something more than the pleasure of hearing a story or of identifying temporarily with an imaginary character. The novel that is no longer centered on an individual, the novel that wants above all to *mean* something, must have recourse to a succession of different kinds of shots. This is the only technical device that allows the novelist both to attain the desired complexity within a continuous narrative and—while maintaining the same objectivity as the cinema—to sufficiently transform the scenes described so as to adapt them to the desired end and make them express the profound meaning of the work.

The essence of film is double, as is that of the god Janus (who would be, by virtue of his presiding over all things transitory and changing, a worthy patron of this supremely fugitive art). On the one hand, cinema is dominated by its desire for hyperreality, because its mechanical means of reproduction encourage it to become more objective than nature itself; but on the other hand, its creator must regain his liberty so that he may leave his mark on the work and raise it to the level of art, and this will be made possible by the camera's mobility, which provides a counterbalance to the hyperobjective method. The contemporary novel tends more and more to the same basic duplicity.

In Proust we already find the recording apparatus being perpetually displaced; in his case, it is displaced in one dimension only—depth. "Perhaps the immobility of the things that surround us is forced upon them by our conviction that they are themselves and not anything else, and by the immobility of our conception of them," he wrote in *Du Côté de chez Swann*.[2] His very personal technique can be interpreted as an effort to make the camera glide along an axis perpendic-

[2] Marcel Proust, *Remembrance of Things Past*, Vol. 1, *Swann's Way*, trans. by C. K. Scott Moncrieff, New York, Random House, 1934, p. 5.—Tr.

ular to the object, ceaselessly moving—often in the course of one single phrase from the surface to the depths—and presenting us not with the diverse appearances of people or things but with "cuts" (similar to the cross-sections used in geology and natural history) made in our perception of them.

A la Recherche du temps perdu thus offers us different cuts made at different moments of time into the reality of the Verdurin salon; the Guermantes way; the personalities of Odette de Crécy, Albertine, and Charlus; the music of Vinteuil; or the narrator's love for Albertine. The cut exposing Swann's response to the Vinteuil sonata at a time when he loves Odette is not at the same depth as the one made by the narrator when, several volumes later, he sees in that sonata a mobile image of eternity. When "Marcel" tires of Albertine because she has pimples on her cheek and no longer makes him uneasy, and when, after her disappearance, he again becomes obsessed by the painful mystery she represents, he is not at the same level, not at the same "stage" of his love. Sometimes he does not get below the surface, below the level of the sociological appearance of a person or a feeling; sometimes, on the contrary, he probes them deeply, dissects their inner structure, describes them almost anatomically. He does not always succeed in uniting these representations, which contradict one another because they belong to different strata of reality.

Because of this perpetual gliding from one level to another, which takes place almost despite himself, he complains at the beginning of *Le Temps retrouvé* (*The Past Recaptured*) of his inability to "observe," in the usual sense of the word— just as a geologist might complain that he does not know how to look at scenery. What my spirit was looking for, he says, and the only thing that could satisfy it,

> —for example, the identical recurrence of the Verdurin salon
> in various times and places—was located halfway down, below

the range of vision, in a zone somewhat recessed. And thus the visible, reproducible charm of people escaped me because I no longer possessed the faculty of confining my attention to it, like the surgeon who, under the glistening whiteness of a woman's abdomen, sees the internal disease gnawing away there. It was of no use for me to go out to dinner, I did not see the guests because, when I thought I was looking at them, I was looking through them as with an X-ray.[3]

This is why he does not recognize "Rachel-Quand-du-Seigneur" in Saint-Loup's beloved, or Elstir in the "Monsieur Tiche" of whom Swann used to speak at an earlier time: he does not see people in the same way as most other men do because the recording apparatus is not situated in him as it is in them. When in one phrase he enumerates all the conceivable reasons for an act without being able to choose one or another, each of the terms of his enumeration constitutes a shot taken of the object from a certain angle and at a certain distance.

What is lacking in Proust's work is not cutting but montage, which would resynthesize these too-diverse views. As Charles du Bos justly says of him, the "three-dimensional world" every novelist creates is for Proust only one of several worlds. His universe, like the filmmaker's, is four-dimensional. Du Bos correctly adds:

> Some of his pages are like the topographical maps in our schoolbooks; and the way in which this geologist of relatively unknown lands eases our passage from one stratum to another suggests a distinctive quality of Proust's genius, agility in depth.[4]

[3] Marcel Proust, *Remembrance of Things Past*, Vol. 2, *The Past Recaptured*, trans. by Frederick A. Blossom, New York, Random House, 1932, p. 888.—Tr.

[4] Charles du Bos, "Approximations, II," trans. by Angelo P. Bertocci, in *From the N.R.F.*, edited by Justin O'Brien, New York, Farrar, Straus and Cudahy, 1958, p. 73.—Tr.

The impression of duration and density given by Proust's work is essentially due to this extreme mobility of the recording apparatus perpetually gliding along its axis.

Despite its multiple perspectives, Proust's narrative remains linear. There is in effect only one recording apparatus, and because it is the eye (or the consciousness) of the narrator, it does not constantly change its nature or direction in relation to the object. The technique is further perfected in Gide's *Les Faux-Monnayeurs*.

As Gide begins to plan his novel, he is already haunted by the question of which point of view to use; he still does not know if he should offer the reader a single or multiple angle of vision:

> The first big question to be examined is this: can I portray all the action of my book through Lafcadio? I do not think so. Probably the point of view of Lafcadio is too narrow to make it desirable to use it all the way through without a break. But what other way is there of presenting *the remainder*? It might be foolish to seek to avoid at all costs the simple impersonal narrative.[5]

He wants to write a complex book, as multiple as life itself; at the same time, as a scrupulous artist, he would like his story to be told by a specific, particular, differentiated person occupying a well-defined place in relation to the events he reports, rather than have it emanate, as it almost always did in the eighteenth century, from an anonymous and falsely objective narrator—a convenient mask for the author. Renouncing his privilege as omniscient creator, he is almost coquettish about not knowing any more about the scenes he describes than the characters who participate in them. He will write, for example: "Bernard and Laura looked at each other, then looked at

[5] André Gide, "The Journal of *The Counterfeiters*," trans. by Justin O'Brien, in *The Counterfeiters*, trans. by Dorothy Bussy, New York, Alfred A. Knopf, 1957, pp. 379–80.—Tr. We know that Lafcadio was originally supposed to have been the main character and moving spirit of the book.

Sophronska; there was a long sigh; I believe it was from Laura." The cinematic technique of changing the position of the recording apparatus will allow him to keep the novel's pluralism while strictly observing his self-imposed convention of always having the recording apparatus situated where a little reflection will enable us to locate it.

Gide also always carefully respects the lighting thrown on his characters, being careful not to describe too precisely a silhouette seen in the distance or to give us details about it we would not be able to see if we were present at the given scene: "Admit that a character who is exiting can only be seen from the rear," he writes in "The Journal of *The Counterfeiters*."[6] This leads to a great complexity of shots. Sometimes we get close-ups: Laura practically falls into Bernard's arms as her chair collapses; we read, "Laura's face was right next to his; he watched her blush," and we effortlessly get the visual transposition of the scene, the close-up of the two faces almost merged into one. At other times Gide uses long shots. Strouvilhou and Laura herself are at first only vague silhouettes passing through the background of the scene; only later are their faces fully illuminated. Gide takes Tolstoy and Martin du Gard to task for not having known how, or not having wanted, to make use of these subtle lighting effects in their works and for having thus given us a vision of things that is too panoramic and lacking in perspective:

> I shall take Martin du Gard to task for the discursive gait of his narrative. His novelist's lamp, wending through the passing years, always illuminates head-on the events he is considering as each one in succession moves into the foreground. Their lives never mingle, and there is no more perspective than there is shadow. This is just what bothers me in Tolstoy. They both paint panoramas; art lies in creating a picture.[7]

[6] Ibid., p. 387.—Tr.
[7] Ibid., p. 384.—Tr.

The characters of *Les Thibault* (*The World of the Thibaults*) are illuminated by a light whose source remains hidden: the author wanted to absent himself from his work with the same inflexible rigor as Flaubert. But because of this too-even lighting, there is no shadow, no relief, no modeling. Gide, on the contrary, only *pretends* to be absent from *Les Faux-Monnayeurs*; he is actually as present as Renoir in *La Bête humaine* or René Clair in *Le Million*. As the director, though he is invisible, he has to be everywhere, if only to regulate the lighting—to throw, for example, a brutal light on the minor characters while allowing the stars to remain in an evocative, shadowy background until the moment when, like Tartuffe or Phèdre in the second act, they are brought into the floodlights. Roger Martin du Gard's art remains above all theatrical, and, as a matter of fact, it is of the theater that his art is born. A rereading of *Jean Barois* makes this obvious, and a more profound analysis of his work (which this is not the place for) will confirm this kinship with dramatic art. All the characters of *Les Thibault* are seen head-on, as in the theater. Those of *Les Faux-Monnayeurs*, however, are shown from many different angles, by a technique so similar to that of the cinema that certain scenes in the book seem ready to be filmed: the scene between Bernard and Laura to which I have previously referred is quite ready to be captured by what Dos Passos calls "the Camera Eye."

Thanks to this technique, Gide was able to achieve one of his basic ambitions: to write a novel that would possess the same complexity as life, that would be, like life, multiple, ambiguous, and continuous—in short, a book whose last sentence could only be the famous "Could be continued." The cutting from one kind of shot to another permits him to succeed where Huxley, in *Point Counter Point*, fails. Despite Huxley's extensive borrowing from Gide (especially the idea of the novel within a novel, Philip Quarles being the super-imposable image of Édouard), Huxley neglected to draw inspiration from the basic narrative technique—a less obvious one, it is true, than the architectural device of weaving the novelist into his own novel. The camera angle—the position of the camera—is constantly shifting in *Point Counter Point*, but the distance between the camera and the object remains stationary. This is exactly the opposite of Proust's method, where it is the distance between the lens and the object that is constantly being changed. Gide, in *Les Faux-Monnayeurs*, achieves the synthesis of these methods, and this double mobility of the camera—in distance and in angle—is what gives his novel this complex pattern, this continuity in the presentation of appearances, which reproduces that of life itself. *Point Counter Point* presents us only with a series of disconnected, flat, one-dimensional pictures whose sequence does not add up to true continuity. Huxley uses a magic lantern, not a camera. His art, like that of Martin du Gard, remains panoramic. Though it is no longer as cramped as the traditional linear narrative of the nineteenth century, it is still incapable of presenting the multidimensional continuity of reality. Like a pointillist painting, *Point Counter Point* sets before the retina of our spirit an assemblage of spots but is unable to integrate them into the living play of light and shadow of the impressionists, Proust and Gide. The American novel learns an analogous lesson from the movies.

After Joyce, the great contemporary master of novelistic technique is Dos Passos.[8] As a matter of fact, the problems he set for himself concern the art of the novel more specifi-

[8] If I had not wanted to limit my examples to contemporary American novelists, I would have enjoyed discussing Henry James's wonderful comments about the technique of the novel—comments which Graham Greene, for example, has known how to profit from.

cally than did Joyce's, whose aesthetic revolution was more oriented toward language in general. What Dos Passos wanted to do in *U.S.A.* was make an epoch and a continent come alive for us by telling a certain number of individual stories. The danger he faced was the possibility of seeing his novel turn into a series of individual monographs, each about one particular character, or—even worse—of seeing the monographs themselves eventually fragmenting into a series of scenes, in which the continuity of each destiny would be lost.

Dos Passos was able to avoid this fragmentation of the book in both space and time by using some of the methods of the cinema, thus restoring to a complex narrative the basic cohesion that the conditions of narrative art tend to deprive it of at every moment. First of all, the characters' biographies interconnect; essentially, it is the same story that is being told in the different parts of the narrative entitled "Eveline Hutchins," "Richard Ellsworth Savage," "J. Ward Moorehouse." But each time the point of view varies, and the camera is inside a different consciousness, that of the character whose name is given to that portion of the narrative. Meanwhile, time goes by, the reel unwinds; we are further along in the film.

As a character's destiny unfolds, his story is told from different points of view. In general, we first see him from his own point of view (the unusualness of the presentation has already been analyzed). Then, once childhood and adolescence have passed and the character has reached the "age of reason" and exists socially, we get the rest of his biography through the eyes of others. For example, in the first two volumes, *The 42nd Parallel* and *1919*, several sections are entitled "Eveline Hutchins" and "Eleanor Stoddard." In the third volume, *The Big Money*, their names do not appear in the table of contents, though they are not absent from the overall fresco Dos Passos wanted to create of America during the period of inflation from 1919 to the crash of 1929. The two heroines are no longer seen in close-up; it is no longer *their* faces that are framed by the klieg lights. This is because they were representative not of postwar America but of the immediately preceding period, which saw them rise to a certain level of society and stop there. Their place is now taken by other characters more typical of this new age of rapid ascents and vertiginous falls: Charley Anderson, the war pilot, becomes a corporation director; Margo Dowling, the model who will become one of the stars of the silent screen; and, finally, Mary French, the young girl of good family who will be converted to militant unionism. Yet we will not be without news of Eleanor, Eveline, and Richard. We will see their silhouettes passing in the background, and we will learn that Eveline was first Richard's mistress, then Charley's, and that she will end up committing suicide by taking an overdose of phenobarbital after giving a brilliant party to which all New York has come to pay her homage; that J. Ward Moorehouse will grow old in solitude, despite his material success; and that Eleanor, who was his mistress, will marry an impoverished Russian prince (she always loved distinction, and her interior decorating business brings in enough money to allow her the supreme luxury—an authentic coronet on her stationery).

The lighting of the characters and their distance from the lens are regulated by the overall perspective: a character will come into the foreground and be filmed in close-up, or he will fade into the background, almost among the extras, according to whether he is more or less representative, more or less symbolic of his time. His silhouette will merge with that of others, borrowed from the most authentic historical reality— for example, Woodrow Wilson or Rudolph Valentino, who have no part in the story but whose exaggeratedly enlarged faces are made for an instant to occupy the foreground of the reader's consciousness by means of the lyrical biographies that momentarily interrupt the action. Cosmic events are unfolded: the war of 1917–18, economic prosperity, the inflation and then the 1929 crash and subsequent crisis, and the advent of talkies. At the same time, the course of individual destinies, in a narration that is always subordinated to the overall design, is also followed. For example, we first hear about the meeting of Eleanor Stoddard (seen in close-up) with J. Ward Moorehouse from her own point of view; we learn about what happens to them while getting the story of Janey, who has become Moorehouse's secretary; the story of Moorehouse's second marriage has been given us through his own biography, and some years later we see, through Janey's eyes, his wife come into the office and create a hysterical scene (we have previously learned through Eleanor that the wife had become a faded blond who never fully recovered from her second pregnancy).

Dos Passos thus indicates that these different stories are important only as parts of a larger whole; the bonds that unite them are as much poetic (or contrapuntal, if you prefer) as novelistic, imbued with a significance that infinitely transcends the relationships that might be established from the purely formalistic point of view of plot alone. The novelist's camera shifts in this work—not constantly (it is still less mobile than that of the movie cameraman), but from one section to another. It shifts, first, each time the author leaves one character to concentrate his attention on another—from Eleanor Stoddard to Charley Anderson, from Eveline Hutchins to "Filette." It also shifts each time he leaves the direct narrative (which is, strictly speaking, novelistic), for one of the nonnovelistic elements, of either poetic or documentary value, with which he has framed it—Newsreels, Camera Eyes, or the biographies of famous men, individuals who symbolize an age.

To retranslate this into the language of film, as even the author's terminology (Newsreels, the Camera Eye) invites us to do, we sometimes have in *U.S.A.* close-ups of real or imaginary people; sometimes (in the Newsreels that express the eddies of the collective consciousness) the "crowd scenes" so beloved of King Vidor or Cecil B. De Mille; or sometimes (in the Camera Eye) the anonymous monologue of a character as representative in his insignificance as are the great men whose personalities are so closely connected with their time—an exact transposition of the cinematic method that consists, in crucial historical scenes, of turning attention away from the hero to fix it on a spectator lost in the crowd, of showing us the gendarme indifferently lighting his pipe while Robespierre's hoarse voice attempts to make itself heard by the hostile crowd on the Ninth of Thermidor, or the tearful face of one of Napoleon's Old Guard during the farewell at Fontainebleau. This method of constructing a novel as a triptych (sometimes as a tetraptych) even uses those "panels" intended to be kept in our minds simultaneously with the central scene, which they frame but do not merge into, recalling the three screens required to project Abel Gance's *Napoleon.*

The technique here is less important than its significance. The distribution of shots into close-ups, middle shots, and long shots reconciles the continuity indispensable to the novel in terms of its story (which is inseparable from the very essence of the genre) with the complexity desired by the author. But this complexity is not an end in itself; Gide's error in *Les Faux-Monnayeurs* was to have taken it as such, so in the final analysis he was incapable of separating his novel from the individuals who were only its supports, not its raison d'être. In Dos Passos the complexity is subordinated to the design of the whole: his trilogy has to be complex because it does not attempt to portray individual destinies but to describe an epoch.

The technique of varying the distance of the camera from the subject enables Dos Passos to create this picture by freeing him from the servitude that had seemed part of the very essence of the novelistic genre: not to be able to describe the impersonal except through and related to the individual. This is the difficulty responsible for the relative failure of Martin du Gard in *Les Thibault* and Jules Romains in *Les Hommes de bonne volonté* (*Men of Good Will*), works analogous to Dos Passos's in intent. Thanks to this technique, the novel is able to attain a reality that surpasses the merely individual; for example, it can lay before us the web of clichés in the mind of an average American or of a member of the New York intelligentsia at the declaration of war in 1917, then can go from this, without abrupt shock, to the vision of a particular person whose exaggeratedly enlarged face reverts, as in the Soviet films, to the anonymity of the close-up. It seems that with the sequence of changes in camera distance, the impersonal novel has found its technique.

It is not surprising that this technique should also be found, in somewhat different forms, in certain French novelists who have pursued an aim similar to that of Dos Passos— those who feel that individual destinies are the materials with which the novelist works, not the central subject of the work (just as, for the painter, colors are the materials, not the objects he wants to reproduce); those who, from Malraux to the Aragon of *Les Cloches de Bâle* (*The Bells of Basel*) and *Les Beaux quartiers* (*Residential Quarters*), and including the Sartre of *L'Age du raison* (*The Age of Reason*) and *Le Sursis* (*The Reprieve*), tell us about a particular incident in a life, then confront it and connect it with an episode in another life, not for its intrinsic interest but so that the impact of these individual stories will give rise to an overall truth that will be the meaning of the novel.

In *La Condition humaine* (*Man's Fate*) Malraux presents us with a series of interrelated scenes that are connected more by aesthetic—almost metaphysical—convergence than by continuity of plot, which is, as a matter of fact, complex and so elliptically presented that few readers can clearly remember it. The point is not so much to tell us the story of the failure of a communist revolution in Shanghai as to set before us a certain total vision of the human condition: to show us what man is capable of; to expose his misery; to describe the dangers that threaten him (Clappique's mythomania, Ferral's will to power, the cruelty of those who suppress the revolution); and, through all of this, to develop an important idea—to illuminate the conditions under which human efforts would have meaning. All this embodied in images of hallucinating precision. The book's scenes are always described from the point of view of one or another of the characters: the author does not appear; the camera is always in the consciousness of a particular person, and the transitions from close-up to long shot are regulated by the oscillations of that person's attention.

Thus, in the opening scenes of the novel the terrorist Ch'en is looking at a man sleeping under mosquito netting, a man whom he must kill but whom he cannot make up his mind to touch. We follow his glance as it moves from place to place like a spotlight, scanning the room, picking out of the shadows first one and then another detail. We are with him when

> his eyes [are] riveted to the mass of white gauze that hung from the ceiling over a body less visible than a shadow, and from which emerged only that foot half-turned in sleep, yet living—human flesh.

> The only light came from the neighboring building—a
> great rectangle of wan electric light cut by windowbars. . . .

There is a noise outside, a traffic jam that turns Ch'en momentarily aside from his vision. Then he is again caught up by
it: "He found himself again facing the great soft smudge of
gauze and the rectangle of light, both motionless in this night
in which time no longer existed.[9]

During the entire scene there is a rhythmic return of the
close-up (the sleeping man's foot); at regular intervals it
hypnotizes us, reinforces our awareness of Ch'en's obsession.
For these few pages we see through Ch'en's eyes. A little
later, having succeeded in killing the man, he enters the
room in which his comrades are assembled, and what he sees
is exaggeratedly enlarged so that it may be impressed upon
us with the obsessional minutiae of a close-up:

> The shutting of the door caused the lamp to swing back and
> and forth: the faces disappeared, reappeared. . . . To the
> right, Kyo Gisors; in passing over his head the lamp accen-
> tuated the drooping corners of his mouth; as it swung away
> it displaced the shadows and his half-breed face appeared
> almost European. The oscillations of the lamp became shorter
> and shorter: Kyo's two faces reappeared by turns, less and
> less different from each other.[10]

At the end of the novel, Gisors's meditations bring us back to
the crucial scenes of the book, again with brusque oscillations
from the close-up to the long shot: "He saw Ferral again,
lighted by the low lamp against the background of the night
full of mist. 'Every man dreams of being God. . . . ' " Then,
immediately after this close-up of Ferral's intense and sharply
illuminated face, we pass to the anonymous noise of the
crowd, exactly as happens in the movies:

[9] André Malraux, *Man's Fate*, trans. by Haakon M. Chevalier, New
York, Random House, 1934, p. 9.—Tr.
[10] Ibid., p. 17.—Tr.

Fifty sirens at once burst upon the air . . . tiny men emerged, like scouts, upon the straight road that led to the city, and soon the crowd covered it, distant and black, in a din of automobile horns. . . .[11]

Malraux does not use this technique only because he has a strong visual imagination; it is bound up with the very essence of his art, with what one might call his *existential* aesthetic. His is always a committed narrative, never an impersonal one; it is always told from *someone's* point of view, in the name of one of the characters. Neither Kyo's death nor the assassination of the man Ch'en kills exists in itself. Because the murder exists for Ch'en and is seen through his eyes, the story of it will partake of the oscillations of his awareness and his vision. Kyo's death exists for May and for Gisors. It is not something abstract; its essence is tied to its method of presentation, and it cannot be separated from it any more than the position of an electron can be considered separately from the observation that reveals it to us. It does not exist except as part of the narrative that is made of it.

Sartre has defined existentialism as the recognition that existence precedes essence in man. In this sense Malraux's work shows a kind of generalized existentialism, since every act as well as every person *is* before it is this or that and since its essence is inseparable from the consciousnesses in which it exists (although there is no question about reducing this essence to the sum of its appearances; this is not the problem). The same holds true for the ethical and metaphysical positions Malraux presents, positions always embodied in a specific character: the different ways in which Kyo and Ch'en and Katov understand the revolution cannot be separated from what they are. None of them is truly distinct from his place in the world or the situation in which he finds himself. Even Gisors, whose function in the novel is to understand

[11] Ibid., p. 358.—Tr.

everything and thus to reestablish a certain harmony in the midst of all this radical pluralism, cannot be considered apart from his opium, his love for Kyo, and, later, his metaphysical passion for music. He *is* all of these things, and it would be false to separate his opinions and his behavior from his *condition*, even in the way they are described.

We can now understand that what has been offered the novelist as a technique for expressing his existential vision of man is a technique allied to that used by the movies, an art form which, more than any other, is *engagé*, inherently incapable of giving us (despite its apparent objectivity) any image that is abstractly impersonal. In a movie, every scene is of necessity photographed from a certain point of view, and this point of view is part of it, inseparable from its essence; it cannot be eliminated to give us a "pure" vision, a vision of someone who would not have a point of view. For centuries human intelligence has been haunted by the dream of a direct apprehension of reality that would be totally objective, one in which the perceiver's physical and psychological structure, his point of view—in short, his *condition*—would not deform and irremediably transform the real into the appearance. This view of the world, to which Bergsonian intuition closely approximates, is very like that which traditional philosophy attributes to the mythical being Joyce calls the "universal knower," more familiarly known as the "philosophers' god." Now, if there is one art forbidden to aspire to such a vision by virtue of its material and its aesthetic essence alike, it must certainly be the one that fragments reality into a disconnected series of appearances: in a movie, all views on the world are legitimate except that of the philosophers' god.

In addition to using the camera's mobility to create foreground and background shots in a narrative, the contemporary novel also makes frequent use of such other cinematic techniques as dolly shots, dissolves, and crosscuts. What is meant by this last is that when two fragments of the same story are developing simultaneously in different places the camera will switch from one to the other. Crosscutting can also be said to occur when this switching is from a contemporary event to one in the past, as in *Le Jour se lève*, where Carné interrupts his narration from time to time to bring us back to the suffocating present—to make the tender idyll coexist with its disastrous conclusion and to seal the love story between the four walls of the room in which Jean Gabin, a hunted man, awaits his capture by the police.

The cinema usually limits itself to crosscutting only two stories or two series of events. The novel can permit itself to interweave many, as in *Point Counter Point, La Condition humaine*, or parts of Jules Romains's *Les Hommes de bonne volonté* series. In one sense the novel has always employed multiple plots, even in Dumas *père* or Eugène Sue: "During this time, the countess, a prisoner in her cell, had not been inactive. . . " but this was only a simple convenience for the story, which was always conceived of as basically linear: at certain times the plot would fragment, would fork, and of necessity force author and reader alike to follow the various fortunes of the different groups of characters separately.

The juxtaposition of tableaux in the modern novel, however, is no longer dictated by plot requirements but is imposed by aesthetic or metaphysical concerns. If Huxley, Malraux, or Jules Romains chooses to tell us several stories simultaneously, it is not always because they are part of the same plot (the events in *La Condition humaine* could unfold quite well without the scene between Ferral and Valérie, and, with just one major exception, without almost all of Baron Clappique's scenes); it is because a certain artistic effect will be created by their juxtaposition. The truth the author wants to communicate will flash out as a result of the mutual impact of these stories in our consciousness, where a mechanism analogous to the one responsible for persistence of vision makes for a residual memory of every scene that has preceded the one we are in the process of reading.

In other cases, the reader is completely aware of the mobility of the recording apparatus; its movement is as evident as that of the camera moving back in a dolly shot to show us a portion of the scene we were hitherto unfamiliar with. The novel often uses a technique similar to that of the dissolve in order to maintain continuity without appearing to lose objectivity. If the author were to move abruptly from one scene to another, we would feel a shock, and this would immediately make us aware of his intervention and destroy the novelistic illusion. Instead of being present at a real story happening in front of our eyes, we would find ourselves in the presence of an imaginary story being told to us by a third person, like the narrator on the radio.

There is an extremely ingenious example of the dissolve in the first chapter of John O'Hara's important novel *Appointment in Samarra*. It is Christmas Eve. In a small midwestern town a married couple, Irma and Lute, are in bed. They have just awakened to make love, and Lute has gone back to sleep. Irma looks at her watch and sees that it is 3:30 A.M. She thinks of the big dance going on at the country club—a dance she and Lute have not been able to attend this year because of lack of money—and hopes that she will be able to go next year:

> If she had married, say, Julian English, she would be a member of the club, but she wouldn't trade her life for Caroline English's, not if you paid her. She wondered if Julian and Caroline were having another one of their battle royals. . . .[12]

And with that the scene changes. The camera glides imperceptibly, and we find ourselves transported, by means of Irma's musings, to the smoking room of the country club, where

[12] John O'Hara, *Appointment in Samarra*, New York, Harcourt, Brace, 1939, p. 9.—Tr.

Julian and Caroline and the others are at this very moment
and where one of the book's crucial scenes is about to take
place.

The current use of crosscuts in the novel has chiefly re-
sulted in the elimination of such anodyne phrases as "During
this time . . . "—phrases which, in the eighteenth- and
nineteenth-century novel (Lesage or Dumas *père*), kept re-
minding us of the obtrusive presence of the narrator. Similarly, the essential innovation of the dissolve is to make the
camera shift imperceptible and thus to allow the passage
from one scene to another without the loss of either the
illusion or the objectivity.

A similar example of this can be found in a scene from
Pierrot mon ami by Raymond Queneau, who consciously imitates the methods of both the movies and the American novel,
especially in *Loin de Rueil* (*Skin of Dreams*). Pradonet, the
owner of the Uni-Park, is surveying the amusements from the
terrace of his house. He sees Pierrot, the hero, taking to his
daughter Yvonne. Without any transition the scene inter-
weaves Pradonet's words with the conversation of the two
young people, as if there had been an abrupt shift of the
recording apparatus—camera or microphone:

> There he is trying to sweet-talk her again. He's got his
> nerve. And what the hell can he be telling her?
> "You don't mind if I talk to you for a while?" Pierre
> asked Yvonne.
> "Of course not," answered Yvonne. "Just the opposite—
> it's nice of you to come see me again . . ."

We then watch the whole flirtation scene and Pierrot's expul-
sion from the grounds from Pradonet's point of view. Once
the scene is over, we become aware that we have not left
Pradonet's consciousness:

> Then all four of them threw him into the night.
> "That's a job well done," said Pradonet, who was follow-
> ing the scene from his terrace. . . .

The importance of this technique, like that of the cross-cut, lies in its elimination of transitions: a new ellipsis, which the cinema has taught the novel. And the point of this ellipsis is not so much to lighten the narrative load significantly by relying on the reader's intelligence as to respect the illusion of hyperreality, which the objectivity of the technique also helps to create. More and more, the anonymous narrator is eliminated from the modern novel; these days he seems as ridiculous as a permanently present narrator commenting on the action in a love or adventure movie. We have finally become aware that each scene in a novel—like each image in a film—bears the imprint of its point of view, has an origin that will make itself sufficiently evident by itself. Every scene in a novel is now understood to be as basically *relative* as a photograph.

Among other novelists the "cutting" has an incomparably faster rhythm. This is true of Aragon and of Elsa Triolet, whose narrative techniques might be defined as much-accelerated Dos Passos. The author of *U.S.A.* proceeds by long sequences: the camera is first placed in J. Ward Moore-house's consciousness, then in Eleanor Stoddard's; in the interval the recording apparatus has registered the newspaper headlines, bits of political speeches, fragments of popular songs, that float around in the collective subconscious of New York, or it has reproduced the interior monologue of an average American, or it has given us a lyrical documentary on Woodrow Wilson or Henry Ford. But each of these sections of the novel remains separate; we always know exactly where we are, and if necessary, the chapter title will tell us. The camera is not as yet very mobile; it remains fixed for long periods, and its movement is discontinuous.

In Aragon's *Les Cloches de Bâle* or Triolet's *Le Cheval blanc* (*The White Charger*), however, the recording instrument is shifting position continuously, and it changes place from phrase to phrase without our being aware of its movement. The reason for this is that a technique directly or indirectly inspired by the movies, and a particular conception of the novel as primarily a narrative, have converged. The essence of a narrative is its continuity. Anyone who has ever told a story to a child knows that the child will always prefer even a naïve and awkward story *told* him by his mother to the most marvelously artistic story that is *read* to him. This is because the personality of the teller, who brings all the disparate elements of the narrative together in one whole, assures a unity of tone to the story that is told, while this same personality, interposing itself between the listener and the story that is being read, constantly tends to break up the unity of the latter.

Aldous Huxley and Jules Romains give us in their novels a succession of tableaux as discontinuous as the sequences of the first silent films; Dos Passos's narrative is continuous only *within* each of the sections that comprise *U.S.A.*, and in *Manhattan Transfer* the fragmentation into scenes is even more evident; with Aragon and Elsa Triolet, however, the novel again becomes primarily an oral narrative. (It was already moving in this direction, thanks to certain artifices that cannot be gone into here, in *Les Faux-Monnayeurs*.) Aragon, in his novels as in his poems, is above all a bard, a worthy successor to the troubadours from whose art he likes to borrow both the poetic themes and the hermetic secrets. In Elsa Triolet, too (as in the great Russian novelists), there is this same narrative gift—this ability to interest no matter whom in no matter what story—which cannot be reduced to anything else.

In addition, these authors almost always tell us what happens, not by means of a neutral narrator but by a sort of chorus—anonymous, to be sure, but not in the least abstract or devoid of personality—someone often involved in the action and always having an opinion about the events he simultaneously comments on and describes. The presence of this chorus that changes as the action changes and is never specifically mentioned is felt only in the way the story is told: when the chorus intervenes, the vocabulary becomes careless, the diction full of clichés. By the flabbiness of the thinking, the mediocrity of the point of view, we recognize that the narrator has been reduced to an emanation of the collective consciousness.

For example, in the second chapter of Aragon's *Les Beaux quartiers* we get a description of Serianne. It begins with a list of particulars made by as impartial an observer as possible, let us say the guide of Serianne, Joanne: "The man who sells funeral wreaths has a store on the market square, next to the branch office of the Banques de Province. . . . " Then the narrator abruptly becomes the embodiment of specific people: it is no longer the guide Joanne who speaks, but this or that busybody or shopkeeper of Serianne. The transformation is marked by the brusque eruption into the sentence of a cliché, a vulgar expression, or a colloquialism: "There's no special day for funeral wreaths, it all depends on the deaths: this second batch is going to butter the bread." (With this cliché the narrator becomes an individual who is no longer limited to describing the topography of Serianne, but also comments on the affairs of the funeral-wreath merchant.) "It's not every month that you're lucky enough to have one of those funerals like old Mme Cotin's, from the Rue Longue, with a bishop no less, but still, good year or bad year, with that little extra at the beginning of November it makes a nice little business, all in all. . . ."

The same is true, in *Les Cloches de Bâle*, of the reaction to Diane's dresses, "through which you could see everything"; the scandalized astonishment that flows so fluently in such a ready-made phrase is probably not the author's. The speaker must be one of the story's anonymous characters whom we have never met directly but whose voice we have heard—a formal, stiff-necked bourgeois or a proper, sharp-tongued old lady (M. or Mme Blin, for instance, or any of their peers chosen at random from among those who frequent Diane's salon but do not approve of her conduct). Without alerting us, the author has shifted his recording apparatus. When it does not merely set a character's behavior or facial play before us, it sometimes captures his interior monologue, sometimes a sociological commentary on his behavior. When Inspector Columbin, who has previously caught Jeanne Cartuywels shoplifting in a large department store, runs into her again, we get a series of close-ups:

> Jeanne's face was pale. . . . Columbin, very much the nice guy, laid his large hairy hand heavily on the fingers of her right hand, which was trembling nervously.
>
> "Come on, don't take it so seriously, we've known each other a long time. . . ."
>
> Large tears had formed on Jeanne's mascaraed lashes. They became heavier, slowly dropped. They fell into the cup, one, two, rippling the coffee. . . .

Almost the entire scene could be transposed into visual images.

This technique differs from the one Dos Passos borrowed from the cinema mainly in this: Dos Passos takes the clichés floating around in the consciousness of the man on the street and creates the quasi-surrealist "collages" called Newsreels; Aragon incorporates these same clichés into the very texture of his story. Their mediocrity, their sloppiness, is so obvious that there is no need to relegate them to a special section of the novel. The narrative retains its continuity, but the illumination of the action changes every minute.

It is the same in *Le Cheval blanc*, which I open at random: "Simone had managed to get Leo Roche out of prison" (objective announcement, indispensable for informing us about the development of events). "It could honestly be said that it was Simone who had procured his temporary liberty" (here begins the chorus of "friends and acquaintances," which comments on Simone's behavior as it reports it). "Simon knew everyone in Paris" (we know this is still the chorus because of the cliché "to know everyone"). "She was full of disconcerting energy. . . . Now that Leo was out of trouble— or almost—Simone began to worry about Michel" (return to the impersonal narrative). "She had neglected him for a long time and he might have found time hanging too heavy on his hands" (Simone's interior monologue, given in the third-person indirect style just as in Dos Passos, even to the cliché "time hanging too heavy on his hands," which shows Simone's lack of cohesiveness and self-awareness). "Lulu, the mannequin, said she had run into him at Fouquet's, Lulu had a soft spot for Michel—it's very simple, she'd never seen such a fine man, and what chic, the sharper the clothes the chicer he was!" (Lulu's words reported by means of Simone's interior monologue).[13]

Here, as in Aragon, there is a different "shot" for each phrase, but continuity is preserved because all of them are translated into spoken language. Raymond Queneau shows the same strange alliance between methods borrowed from an art that appears to be essentially visual in nature, like the cinema, and a technique that restores to the novel its narrative essence and makes it more than ever an art of language.

Actually, this alliance is perhaps less strange than it at first seems. If a single work can borrow from the cinema and from spoken language at the same time, it is because the

---

[13] Elsa Triolet, *The White Charger*, trans. by Gerrie Thielens, New York, Rinehart & Company, 1946, p. 291.—Tr.

novel, like the film, is basically narrative. As the first chapter of this book makes clear, the multiple analogies between the novel and the movies can be explained by the fundamental aesthetic relationship between the two genres. The moviegoer, like the novel reader, is alone, face to face with his dream just like every one of the listeners hypnotized each night by the Arabian storyteller—face to face with his dream as incarnated in Scheherazade or Sinbad, Marlene Dietrich or Julien Sorel.

It would be wrong to try to explain the reciprocal borrowing between the film and the novel[14] or between the French novel and the American novel by the vague concept of "influence." It is difficult to speak of imitation or even of transposition if by that is meant an actual historical process. The preceding sections of this book lead rather to a theory of *convergence* between arts that are different in nature and in country of origin. In an earlier book, *Les Sandales d'Empédocle*, I suggested that literary critics (among others) take on the task of bringing to light this kind of convergence by the analysis (if not the psychoanalysis) of themes common to artists of the same period. At that time I was thinking especially of analogies in the content, the *message*, of works very different in form—like the convergence it is easy to establish between Franz Kafka and Henri Michaux or between the latter and Evelyn Waugh.

The similarities of *technique* in the film, the American novel, and the French novel are, however, perhaps even more suggestive. In any event, they throw light on the nature of the influence one literary genre, one artistic domain, can have on another. It is as if truths, no less than aesthetic forms, could be dated: one and the other are immersed in history.

---

[14] Since a movie like *Citizen Kane* is obviously (if not grossly) influenced by the American novel, especially by the techniques of Dos Passos, the cinema would seem to get its own back from the novel.

This is why an idea or an artistic innovation that scandalizes one period is accepted without question—and almost seen as a platitude or a truism—some years later. No matter how original the creator is, we should not underestimate his dependence on the time in which he lives: he is bound by his era. The similarities everyone has noted between Bergson's work and Proust's (despite the protestations of the latter) are undoubtedly much more explicable by a common dependence on the same epoch, the same state of society, than by actual influence. They resemble each other to the extent to which they both partake of the "mentality" common to their time.

But it is possible that one artistic form may be better adapted to an era than others contemporary with it. The explanation for the current popularity of the American novel in France is probably that its role, in relation to French literature, is as much that of *precursor* as of example—which is the same relationship the film has to the novel. Both the movies and the American novel are in advance of European works, and the reasons for this advance position are the same in both cases: a new literature necessarily outpaces an older literature, weighed down by an inert mass of traditions that must constantly be renewed from within, just as popular art outpaces subtle, esoteric art because it is more immediately in tune with the hidden sensibility of the masses and the changes it is undergoing.

When a new aesthetic need is expressed and satisfied by an art that springs up in response to it, it can seem as if the other arts, evolving at a slower pace, are borrowing its methods, even if there has been neither direct influence nor conscious imitation. But reflection on the pseudo-resemblances might hasten the evolution, direct it by making it conscious. One cannot pretend, for instance, that the novel has learned the multiple uses, aesthetic and metaphysical, of the ellipsis from the movies. Balzac and Flaubert knew the value of ellipsis just as Stendhal and Maupassant knew the value of an absolutely objective narration. But the example, the closeness, of an art in which language must necessarily play a subordinate role will not be lost on the novelist; it will remind him that his chosen genre must not lose itself in a flood of words that can only dilute the aesthetic intensity, and that the best chance of achieving a more fully adequate relationship between thought and expression will come, thanks to ellipsis, from "negative values."

Recognition of the kinship between the narrative of the novel and the narrative of the film gives us a deeper understanding of their essence and of the aesthetic laws that govern them. A movie is a series of images, and a story is a succession of phrases, both sequences being so ordered as to form a continuous narrative, each having the capacity for as much complexity as is desired. Now, a story always presupposes a narrator, but a narrator can be changed during the course of the work as often as one wishes (as in Faulkner and Aragon), and with no obligation on the part of the author even to alert the reader to the change—*provided that there always be a narrator*, a convention made necessary by the very essence of the genre. The error of naturalism is to have believed that the story would be more objective precisely to the degree that the narrator could be made more neutral, more impersonal.

And even this error is instructive. In literature, as in metaphysics, the nineteenth century still believed in the possibility of arriving at a universal, absolute truth, valid for all men. Zola's aesthetic rests on exactly the same error as the conception of "scientific" history found in Charles Seignobos and Langlois, a conception that Péguy, who had so strong a sense of temporality, long ago demolished. In philosophy it needed the epistemological reflections of A. S. Eddington and Raymond Aron, and in metaphysics, the whole current of existentialism, to teach man to disassociate the true and the absolute—those two values much too precipitately identified by the nineteenth century—and make him admit that relativism is not necessarily synonymous with skepticism.

The double example of the movies and the American novel has rendered an analogous service to literature by demonstrating that a story, like a thought, must always have a specific and involved person behind it. The whole difference between the art of Martin du Gard, a man of the nineteenth century as much by his technique as by his metaphysics, and that of the novelists of truly modern spirit, like Aragon and Malraux, stems from the latter group's recognition of (at least implicit) and meditation on this truth. Thus, the technique of using different kinds of shots, as well as the "hyperobjective" method of description, have profound significance: thanks to them, the novelist communicates—by the very texture of his narrative, without any need for abstract explanations—the idea that every observer has his own point of view, that every person is in a particular place. He sets before us a truth already latent in the works of Proust and Gide: any statement about a character varies in relation to the angle of the view and the distance from the subject.

We are here concerned with a new convergence of the same kind as that which has already been discussed—a convergence between the results of psychoanalysis, behaviorism, and sociology and the new vision of the world that the movies and the novel communicate to us almost unconsciously, by virtue of their technique alone. It is no longer a question of a kinship between two forms of the same genre or of two neighboring arts, but of one between the abstract themes that haunt contemporary thought and the conclusions that are suggested by the evolution toward an epoch of purely aesthetic techniques belonging to the domain of the emotions rather than of the intellect. This is a partial explanation of the growing vogue for the American novel in France: it was the first to know how to give literary expression to tendencies so profound that only those few capable of abstract reflection had become aware of them. In an obscure and often confused way, it has made certain truths immediately perceptible to everyone, and this very obscurity has enabled it to diffuse these truths more widely than could have been done by a philosophic essay.

But this is not the only reason for its success: it also gives us a more simple and direct, and therefore a more universal, vision of man than that proposed by our traditional literature. Through its masterpieces we glimpse the promise of a new humanism. If its major importance is its content, however, why is it its technique that is most imitated? To use Sartre's apt phrase, it is because the technique is pregnant with a whole metaphysic. Even more, it is a means of communicating this metaphysic directly to the reader by addressing itself to the "sensitive part" of his soul—a means of making him acknowledge a truth in a more immediate, more emotional, more peremptory fashion than by subjecting him to dialectical exercises or abstract reflection.

PART TWO

Time and
Impersonalism in
the American Novel

5 *Dos Passos's* U.S.A., *or the Impersonal Novel*

Eisenstein, it seems, wanted to make a movie about Capital. The novel about Capital, which both Zola and Upton Sinclair had tried in vain to write, has been brought off by Dos Passos in *The Big Money*, the third volume of *U.S.A.* The image of the modern world that neither *L'Argent* nor *Oil!* succeeds in placing before us in a convincing manner, that only the prophetic genius of Balzac has given us some hints of, we get from the author of *Manhattan Transfer*, who makes it loom before us by means of an ensemble of complex techniques—of unequal value—worked out and worked over for fifteen years. The publication of *The Big Money* was a double event: the book marked a stage in the evolution of the contemporary novel toward an ever more impersonal art, and, in terms of Dos Passos's own development, it marked the moment in which he attained both a full awareness of what he wanted to say and a perfect mastery of the way in which to say it. It is therefore now possible to indicate the limits of this kind of art.

In Europe, the novel has for quite some time been moving in the direction of impersonalism, though quite timidly. The traditional narrative centered on a specific character— Adolphe, Dominique, the Princess of Cleves, Moll Flanders, Henry Esmond, Daniel Deronda—has increasingly been giving way to a new type of novel whose subject, and even manner, are supplied by a collective reality. This change can be documented in very simple and unsubtle ways—for example, by book-title statistics: novels are less and less frequently named for their heroes. Titles like *Rachel, Lucienne, Diana of the Crossways, Adrienne Mesurat,* have become rare; *The Magic Mountain* is not called "Hans Castorp," nor *La Nausée* (*Nausea*) "Antoine Roquentin." Even if the author calls his work by the name of the central character, as in *Jean-Christophe,* that character is more the Vergil who guides us through this new and human comedy than the favored subject or the connecting thread that binds together all the episodes. The hero's consciousness is simply the point of view selected by the author for the contemplation of the reality he wants to portray; the title of the book is the road marker, the topographical indicator, that locates the chosen observatory.

In Europe this new type of impersonal novel has given us the story of a family—the Thibaults, the Buddenbrookses, the Pasquiers, the Forsytes; or the description of an atmosphere—*The Magic Mountain* or *Dusty Answer;* or sometimes, as in *Les Hommes de bonne volonté,* a more ambitious overall design, but one that becomes no clearer with the appearance of each succeeding volume. In America, however, the novel has become the story of a collective entity—more frankly, more deliberately, and more consciously than was attempted in France even by Unanimism.

With John Dos Passos the novel openly takes as its subject a latitude *(The 42nd Parallel),* a date *(1919),* a sociological era—that of America during the industrial upsurge that followed the 1914–18 war *(The Big Money)*; Steinbeck uses a fruitpickers' strike as his subject in *In Dubious Battle*. *(Ulysses* had already given us the story of a day in the city of Dublin rather than of the adventures of Leopold Bloom or Stephen Daedalus—an effort to paint the collective soul of the city and to reconstruct for us, on a larger scale than Jules Romains had dared in *Puissances de Paris*, the rhythmic pulse of a city during twenty-four hours.[1]) Sometimes the critic is hard put to explain the precise nature of this non-human being that is the center of the novel, though he is perfectly aware of its existence. Who could define the impersonal reality that forms the subject of *Sanctuary*? But generally speaking, the American novel, simpler in design than the French novel, lends itself better than the latter to analysis: it tends to be the portrayal of a purely collective reality, while French attempts to arrive at something that transcends the individual quickly veer toward the expression of a metaphysical rather than a social reality—for example, Louis Guilloux's *Le Sang noir (Bitter Victory)* and Malraux's *La Condition humaine*.

These new aspirations and this change of viewpoint have obliged the novel to abandon traditional techniques and create new means of expression. Dos Passos's work represents the most systematic efforts in this direction. Still hesitant in *Manhattan Transfer*—an odyssey of New York just as *Ulysses* is

[1] Frank Budgen's *James Joyce and the Making of Ulysses* (Bloomington, Indiana, Indiana University Press, 1960 [originally published in 1934]) confirms this. While writing *Ulysses*, Joyce told Budgen one day: "I want to give a picture of Dublin so complete that if the city one day suddenly disappeared from the earth it could be reconstructed out of my book" (pp. 67–68). A reading of *Ulysses* will show how well he realized this ambition.

of Dublin—he is in full command of his new technique in the great trilogy *U.S.A.*, especially in the third volume.

And yet his first books showed hardly any signs of going beyond the usual ambitions of the novel. In the most classic as well as the most banal sense of the term, there is a "hero" in each of his first two published works: Martin Howe in *One Man's Initiation*, and John Andrews in *Three Soldiers*. Even so, the interest in the latter book was first centered, as the title indicates, on a group of three men, each of whom embodies a different type of American: Fuselli, a Westerner; Christfield, a Southerner; and John Andrews, a musician from New York. The author undoubtedly planned to schematize by their trinity the complexity and multiformity of the American army, but his fidelity to this initial design is almost involuntary. All the characters, even the peripheral ones, seem to evaporate into anonymity, interchangeability. Despite its title, *Three Soldiers* is really the story of only one man, John Andrews, who—as is proper for the hero of a novel—resembles the author like a brother and makes a very individual claim on our sympathy and pity. Even his being an artist—a hypersensitive and creative being—is significant, and the transposition of the writer into the musician is transparent.

This intimate relationship of tender consubstantiality between the author and his hero is also found in *Manhattan Transfer's* Jimmy Herf; but here the proportion of impersonal elements has noticeably risen, and the reader has to make an effort of critical reflection to perceive that Jimmy is still the central character—the only character except for Ellen who is not peripheral, the only one in whose favor the author mobilizes our sympathy. In one sense, however, in this book as in *Three Soldiers*, there are two characters, two entities, confronting each other: Jimmy and the modern world in this book, John Andrews and the monstrous bureaucratic war machinery that ends by crushing him in *Three Soldiers*.

U.S.A. is completely different. The Sacco-Vanzetti case triggered an abrupt crystallization of Dos Passos's message and his art. This time no character can qualify as a hero, either because of the central place he occupies or because of his resemblance to his creator, whose secret predilection for him is almost involuntarily communicated to us. Only Richard Ellsworth Savage is perhaps momentarily a candidate for this privileged position, but the very narrative method the author has chosen obliges him to objectivity, externality, and impartiality. Destroying by his method the fragile umbilical bond that occasionally seeks to establish itself, Dos Passos has to describe Dick, as well as every other character, in terms and from a point of view rather reminiscent of those Sartre uses to portray his *salauds*. This is because the Sacco-Vanzetti case (which explicitly or implicitly occupies the entire last third of *The Big Money*) came as a rude awakening to Dos Passos. The affair precipitated, in the chemical sense of the word, what was thereafter to be Dos Passos's conception of society—a conception of two nations, two Americas, boldly confronting each other at the end of *U.S.A.*, a conception admirably expressed in the following lyrical monolgue (as well as elsewhere):

> They have clubbed us off the streets   they are stronger they are rich   they hire and fire the politicians the newspaper editors the old judges the small men with reputations the collegepresidents the wardheelers (listen businessmen collegepresidents judges   America will not forget her betrayers) they hire the men with guns the uniforms the policecars the patrolwagons
>   All right you have won   you will kill the brave men our friends tonight . . . all right we are two nations. . . .[2]

[2] John Dos Passos, *The Big Money*, Boston, Houghton Mifflin, 1946, pp. 537–38.—Tr.

Or again, in the book's final closing vision—as important for
the poetic and metaphysical significance of the whole as the
last image of a movie or the final "Yes" of Molly Bloom's
monologue in *Ulysses*—entitled "Vag," there is the monologue
of Vag, the hungry boy, having neither home nor hearth,
who, from the side of the road on which he is dragging his
bleeding feet and his wretched cardboard valise, looks up at
the plane carrying prosperous and well-fed businessmen
across America.

Before *U.S.A.* Dos Passos's characters opposed society in
much the same way the romantic hero had—as individuals
and even, insofar as they were artists, as superindividuals. In
the symbolic ending of *Three Soldiers*, where John Andrews
is carried off to prison while the sheets of his great opera,
The Queen of Sheba, float off in the wind, it is as a creative
artist that he is destroyed, overwhelmed by the social machine. In the same way, Jimmy Herf's fight, because it is
individualistic, remains romantic and erratic—therefore inef-
ficacious. Here we have not one man pitting himself against
society, but two societies, two Americas—the workers and the
exploiters, the haves and the have-nots—confronting each
other. Hemingway shows the same kind of development: his
unsuccessful novel *To Have and Have Not* represents the
turning point in his evolution from the romantic and almost
Byronic individualism of *A Farewell to Arms* to the more
tranquil impersonalism of *For Whom the Bell Tolls*.

A profound transformation of Dos Passos's style takes
place simultaneously with the change of message. The writing in *Manhattan Transfer* uses techniques very similar to
those used by Joyce in *Ulysses*, which is its obvious inspiration. The two books are connected even by the use of those
author's "doubles," Jimmy Herf and Stephen Daedalus—heroes
who are sympathetic and pitiable in and because of their
weakness—both of whom are seen from within. (No one is

ever strong in his own eyes, and Balzac had to show De Marsay and Vautrin from the outside to preserve their prestige.) The technique of *U.S.A.* is, on the contrary, so profoundly original that it has a posterity instead of an ancestry. (Even in France it inspired Sartre—perhaps more when he was not consciously aware of it, as in *L'Enfance d'un chef* [*The Childhood of a Leader*], than when he was fully aware of it, as in *Le Sursis.*) The technique is newer and more fecund because of its subtle and hidden methods of narration and character presentation than because of the more obvious overall structure of the book—brought to a point of perfection in *The Big Money.*

The first impression of any part of *U.S.A.*—*The Big Money,* for example—suggests that the author has not so much profoundly modified the texture of the novelistic narrative as he has framed and surrounded it with extra-novelistic elements, like the Newsreels. If what he really wanted to write was the story of a collective entity, as the titles of his books lead us to believe, it seems as if he did it by juxtaposing bits of stories that could all have belonged to old-fashioned novels centered on individuals. For example, in *The Big Money,* the stories of Charley Anderson, Margo Dowling, and Mary French could be pieced together, labeled with the name of its protagonist, and put end to end, thus forming two or three nearly autonomous short novels or long short stories: those of Charley and Margo come together for a moment when Margo becomes Charley's mistress after his divorce, but Mary's story intrudes as little as possible into that of the two others.

In the same way the contents of this volume seem at first sight to have little connection with that of the two preceding ones. Only Charley is previously known to us, and when we open this third volume for the first time we are disappointed at not "finding out what happened" to Dick Savage, Eveline

Hutchins, and Eleanor Stoddard—characters we became involved with in the two earlier novels. Yet we are not without news of them: by a method rather analogous to that used by Jules Romains in *Les Hommes de bonne volonté*,[3] the characters' destinies intersect, though briefly, hardly more than would happen in real life; the outline of a character we are familiar with passes through the story we are in the process of reading just like a woman passing through a room. We see Eveline Hutchins through the eyes of Charley, whose mistress she is for a short time, and at the end we learn, through Mary French, who has gone to a reception at her home the night before, that she has committed suicide. Similarly, from the moment Margo Dowling becomes a Hollywood star, we learn nothing more of her directly; only in the last episode, centered on Mary French, do we learn about the final failure of her career because her voice is not suited to the new talkies. From this point of view it would seem as if the new formula for the novel consists of juxtaposing and loosely connecting two or three traditional novels.

But the requirements of verisimilitude make it impossible to complicate indefinitely the plot of such a vast trilogy and then to have all the characters meet in the last volume as if it were the fifth act of a comedy. In addition, because each of these stories is told from the viewpoint of the character whose name it carries—a monad whose perspective we temporarily identify with that of the universe—the novel remains compartmentalized, cellular; it is not the description of a reality shared by all.

Dos Passos could not limit himself to traditional technique because it employs only people—individuals—as raw

[3] When, for example, Jallez is about to visit, at Digne, the Abbé Mionnet, who has become a bishop, or when we are told in the course of the weekend Germaine Baader and Henry Mareil spend at Celle-les-Eaux about the success of Haverkamp's enterprises.

material or pawns, so he interwove the stories centered on people, which constitute the narrative thread of his books, with literary fragments of an entirely new form. Sometimes these are Newsreels with newspaper headlines: "COLONEL HOUSE ARRIVES FROM EUROPE," "THREE CROOKS KILL A MAN A FEW FEET AWAY FROM THE HOTEL MAJESTIC," "JOBLESS FIGHT IN AN EMPLOYMENT AGENCY." Sometimes there are fragments of political speeches, articles, advertisements: "tired of walking, of biking, of taking buses, he will probably buy a Ford . . . "; "young man wanted. . . ." Sometimes there are bits of popular songs: "Yes, We Have No Bananas," or "Saint Louis Blues." The Newsreels present, in short, everything that gives an age its specific historic color, all the anonymous debris that floats around in the consciousness of the man in the street, the man in the subway—the man who reads his paper or glances at his neighbor's, or who vaguely remembers, to the rhythm of his walk or the jolts of the bus, bits and pieces of what he has seen and heard during the day. These Newsreels constitute the completely impersonal monologue of the collective unconscious, of Heidegger's *Mann*, of everyman; of "no matter who goes from here to there . . . " as Jules Romains's Vorge sings.

Sometimes this disembodied monologue fixes itself. It goes on in one consciousness, becomes precise and particular while still remaining anonymous; it draws into its current, integrates into its texture, the well-defined circumstances of a life that is banal, to be sure, but also differentiated. It is no longer the subconscious inner monologue of a subway crowd, but the supraliminal one of an individual who is part of that crowd. The novelist's camera becomes the eye of an individual human being, from whence the name given to these fragments —the Camera Eye.

Finally, there are Whitman-like poetic biographies, almost always attaining an epic grandeur, which spotlight a figure particularly representative of a moment, a period, an aspiration. Sometimes this biography is of a man who at a certain moment steps into the limelight (like Woodrow Wilson in 1918); sometimes, of someone who is, like Henry Ford or Fred Taylor, the creator of a whole new era; sometimes, of a personality who is simply the symbol of that era, like Rudolph Valentino and Isadora Duncan, who in *The Big Money* incarnate the collective aspirations concentrated on the unreal, glamourous world of the movies and the dance.

All these nonnovelistic elements are rigorously connected thematically to the personal stories they interrupt and accompany. An attentive reading of the first pages of *The Big Money* is enough to make clear the numerous correspondences between the first narrative chapter and, for example, the Newsreels that immediately follow it. As in an operatic overture, the basic themes of the book are announced: the cheerful, typically American complacency and self-satisfaction as expressed, for example, in Paul Johnson's cliché as he is about to get off the ship ("Well, we're back in God's country"); the gigantic campaign to boost the idea of prosperity after the first world war;[4] the muzzling of the workers by the trusts;[5] and the moral disintegration of returning soldiers. (As Ollie Taylor says in the first chapter: "We could stand the war, but the peace has done us in!"; this is echoed by a news story: "The only survivors of the schooner *Onato* are put in jail on arrival in Philadelphia.")

As in Joyce, the reader's unconscious is prepared to *hear*

[4] "but has not the time come for newspaper proprietors to join in a wholesome movement for the purpose of calming troubled minds, giving all the news but laying less stress on prospective calamities" [Ibid., p. 10].

[5] "they permitted the steel cartel to trample underfoot the democratic rights which they had so often been assured were the heritage of this country" [Ibid., p. 10].

the story; the characters' changes of consciousness—which might have passed unperceived—are underlined by echoing them in the Newsreels. In short, the author makes sure that none of the themes will be lost from sight, no matter how great the complexity of the ensemble, by means of the same procedure followed by Joyce in *Finnegans Wake*: by repeating twenty times in different ways the truths one wants to communicate to the reader—truths that are actually quite simple in themselves, but which might be difficult to apprehend because of their plurality and interconnection. This technique allows Dos Passos to preserve in his book one of the essential aspects of novelistic pleasure—that of cursory and almost absentminded reading.

The American critic Harry Levin has very subtly observed that the difficulty in *Finnegans Wake* is only apparent: the same tricks are used so many times and superimposed on the mind of the reader in so many ways that everyone—even someone leafing through the book without any special concentration, or someone who occasionally allows his attention to wander—will nevertheless retain the essential. Thanks to this hammering away, to this insistence, Dos Passos is able to enlarge his reader's field of consciousness and communicate to him simultaneously—without causing him excessive fatigue and without destroying his naïve novelistic pleasure—the diverse elements of his polyphony. In *The Big Money*, Dos Passos's aesthetic, like Joyce's, is an aesthetic of redundancy.

The thematic construction allows him to resolve another difficulty, one created for the novelist—as for the practitioner of every other language art—by the discontinuity inherent in the narrative, which is the reason for the multiplicity and disparity of his "shots." Thus, in *The Big Money* Margo Dowling leaves for Havana with the young Cuban good-for-nothing she has just married. The novelist moves his recording apparatus first to the consciousness of a tourist about to embark, and then to that of an emigrant—a steerage passenger—who is also going south. We do not follow Margo during her trip, but we are not cheated of the time it takes for her to make it: the passage of time will be beaten out for us by the unfolding of the impressions of this anonymous consciousness. As Sartre so profoundly observed, Dos Passos's characters are only minimally at home in their own consciousnesses: they are not comfortable with themselves; it is as though they have no inner being. The switch from the personalized and novelistic narrative to the Camera Eye reinforces this impression: the individuality of each character's consciousness vacillates, then suddenly fades into anonymity.

We are now prepared to understand why Margo's response to her pregnancy is passive, why her in-laws are hostile, why her husband is indifferent—and why, one fine day and without any apparent reason, she abruptly gives up this existence that had only so provisionally nested in her. Her later existence as a famous star is equally provisional, just as first the material success of Charley Anderson and then his reverses of fortune also take up successive residence in *his* "personality," in his "consciousness" (in Dos Passos's world these words can only be used with quotation marks) without his ever having belonged to them, without their ever having been part of him, without his ever having had full possession of the things that happened to him, without his ever having been able to accept these events, assume responsibility for them, or integrate them—even as accidents—into his being.

The use of the Camera Eye thus draws attention to certain aspects of the narrative that might otherwise have escaped us. After this unfolding of the states of consciousness of an individual, personalized character in whom we have momentarily become interested, the interior monologue of his anonymous "double" takes up, in a mocking counterpoint, the same themes and shows the same preoccupations. Similarly, the Newsreels—with their web of clichés, advertising slogans, and ephemeral magic words—enable us to discover, in the inner discourse of the characters, the same clichés and the same slogans, playing in relation to these characters the role of a photographic "developer" and underlining for us their profound lack of individuality and their nonexistence. Though they are on a different level, the nonnovelistic elements are strongly connected with the story. They not only frame the story, but the story takes on its true significance and acquires its multiple dimensions only when seen in their perspective.

A closer look at the technique employed in the actual narrative shows that it only *seems* traditional. The tone in which the various stories are told, the grammatical tenses and times, and the vocabulary used in the narration are all quite unusual. Dos Passos did indeed choose to use the preterit[6]— the best tense for expressing things in the process of happening—but in his hands this traditional tense becomes a means of telling a very special kind of story: the way in which a character would describe his life, tell what has happened to him, if he were talking to a friend, to a third person interposed between self and self, between himself as actor and himself as narrator. He describes himself objectively, in the third person, a little as if his life were being projected on a screen; but the proof that his is not an entirely objective narration, in terms of behavior, is that he is aware of things that only he can know: his feelings, his worries, his emotions. It must therefore certainly be he who is speaking; the recording ap-

---

[6] And not the imperfect, like Flaubert in certain parts of *L'Education sentimentale*; the past definite, like Camus in *L'Etranger*; or the present, like Damon Runyon in his stories about racketeers—three unusual tenses the authors used in hopes of creating a definite effect. The external syntactical form of Dos Passos's narration in *U.S.A.* is, on the surface, classical.

paratus—which is, instead of ordinary introspection, a "lens" in the true sense of the term—is in his consciousness. He limits himself to *recounting*, without explaining or analyzing: it would not be natural to go in for long, drawn-out explanations for a friend. His experience is expressed in terms of the world of ready-made ideas and conversational clichés: Janey's relationship with G. H. Barrow is described in the slang of a young girl: "She kidded him a good deal and she thought maybe he was getting a crush on her, but he was the sort of man who'd be like that with any woman."[7] This is exactly, except for the use of the third person, what she would say to a friend in describing her flirtation. In the same way, when Eleanor thinks about her relationship with J. Ward Moore-house, she does not analyze her feelings for him at all; the real content of her consciousness (which the incisive analysis of the traditional novel would uncover but which never appears in Dos Passos) is hidden from her, and from us, behind the mask of sentimental clichés—exactly the ones she would use with Eveline or anyone else she might confide in.[8]

Dos Passos's characters are not on intimate terms with themselves. When Eleanor goes to J. W.'s wife to persuade her that she, Eleanor, has only a Platonic relationship with him, she uses the same expression she had used earlier when telling herself that the friendship was "as pure as driven snow." The harmony of the characters' inner speech and their spoken words does not keep them from being profoundly

[7] Note the schoolgirl clichés Dos Passos uses, especially "kid" and "crush"; the use of "maybe," which belongs to spoken language; and finally, the magnificent "idée reçu" that would have rejoiced Flaubert —a "man who'd be like that with any woman."

[8] "Eleanor often thought it was a shame J. W. had such a stupid wife who was an invalid too, but she thought the children were lovely and it was nice that they both had lovely blue eyes like their father." [John Dos Passos, *The 42nd Parallel*, Boston, Houghton Mifflin, 1946, p. 408.]

insincere[9] even when they think themselves most honest; sincerity is impossible for them because they *are* actually nothing but bundles of ready-made opinions and ideas they have received—together with their vocabulary—from one or another social group. And this is the reason for Dos Passos's insistence on the physical aspects of existence—the only authentic stock-in-trade of these beings who are so completely absorbed by the social. Hunger, exhaustion, lack of money, sexual dissatisfaction, hangovers, insecurity in all its forms, fear of sickness, pills to bring on menstruation—these details and sordid experiences are what make up the true "inner life" of his characters.

It is also significant that the novelist abandons his characters as soon as they meet with some success, in no matter what area. This is particularly clear in *The Big Money*, in which we learn practically nothing about Charley and absolutely nothing about Margo during their prosperity (and, for that matter, nothing about their sexual or romantic affairs when *they* are going well, either).[10] This is because the character returns during this period to the complete anonymity of success: Charley is nothing more than a designer of planes, Margo only one star among many others. The individual is completely reabsorbed into the collective; only failure will make him stand out again. The sole reality of Dos Passos's characters derives from their suffering, their unsatisfied desires, their consciousness of pain—like the consciousness of an unhappy animal whose dark night of instinct is occasionally illumined by a flash of lucidity. In man, who is more com-

---

[9] As a matter of fact, in the next volume we discover, through the eyes of Eveline Hutchins and with the same astonishment she feels, that J. W. has slept with Eleanor.

[10] Yet it is not objectively true that happy people have no story. For someone who truly exists, happiness is a series of experiences at least as valid as suffering. As a matter of fact, it is possible to speak of a certain monotony of unhappiness.

plex, the anguish lasts longer; but when it stops, the light goes out. We are not shown Charley Anderson happy in Dora's arms (and this is one of the principal uses of those previously mentioned ellipses in Dos Passos's art—arbitrary, to be sure, but also legitimate in the literary work they shape), or Eveline Hutchins finally meeting the lover who fulfills her expectations. In Dos Passos's story she is never seen except as tormented by an unsatisfied sensuality or bothered by her ignorance of birth control: only at these moments does the author see her as truly existing. Eleanor Stoddard's reality is not, as she undoubtedly believes it to be, that she loves Rodin and Whistler; it is that she owes money to her furrier, and that she has a sick and almost psychotic horror of everything dirty or bloody. The reality of Agnes, Margo Dowling's stepmother, is not that she has pure thoughts conforming to the theories of Christian Science but that she is an excellent housekeeper and, since she cannot have children of her own, sincerely and tenderly loves Margo.

The lack of a basic reality in Dos Passos's characters explains their curiously vacillating nature, which is one of the things that most strikes—and perhaps shocks—us on first reading. We notice, for example, the ease with which they make decisions, accept—without understanding why—a job or a woman they will leave shortly thereafter with just as little reason, and drift through life at the mercy of events or of their momentary impulses—as if there were in them neither ambition nor will nor anything permanent, not even what traditional psychology calls "character." The perfect example of this is Charley Anderson, who on the eve of his marriage to Anne, after long being attracted to her, allows himself to be seduced, in the strictest sense of the word, by a sudden desire he feels for Gladys.

In all of these beings there is a strange superficiality: it is as if they have only two dimensions; as if they lack depth, con-

tinuity; as if they are minus the indispensable link that con-
nects (at least so we have been taught and so we believe)
our states of consciousness and our acts with the mysterious
core of the individual—what we call "personality." Each of
them seems to "play" his life, in the triple sense of the word:
like a child, like an actor, like an habitué of a gambling casino.
It does not really seem to belong to him. His success or failure
is equally an accident, that is, the result of statistical chance,
independent of his true nature. Thus, Charley makes a fortune, then loses all his money—is first swept along by the
boom, then ruined by the Depression. Thus, Eveline Hutchins
marries because Paul Johnson has made her pregnant. Thus,
Margo becomes a star because a somewhat fanatical photog-
rapher, now a great director, is one day infatuated with her
face. There is no connection between the various events that
constitute a biography, or any intelligible relationship between
these events and the true being (in any case nonexistent) of
the character. The novel of people dispossessed of themselves
—that is what Dos Passos's trilogy is. If they were more lucid,
if they were even simply presented as *conscious*, one might
say of them that they are "absurd," in Camus's sense of the
word. But they live in an absurd world, and they are not
aware of it. They may complain, but they are never surprised.
The absurd is within them: they do not see it.

Despite this absurdity, or perhaps because of it, even
their encounters—by their intrinsic absurdity and fortuitous
importance—often evoke Lucretius' image of the collision of
atoms: blind, reasonless, incoherent, but nevertheless capable
of overturning everything and ultimately creating a world,
fashioning a life. Analogous comments could be made about
the characters of other American novelists—those, for example, of John O'Hara's admirable *Appointment in Samarra*.

Their creators thus manage to communicate a very special kind of malaise, one we sometimes get, though to a lesser

degree, from the magazine stories so useful in studying both the psychology and the sociology of American life. In these stories the characters are cliché-ridden—true social manne- quins clothed in platitudes and satisfied to be so—and all the more terrifying because they do not have even the relative existence suffering confers on the emptiest of consciousnesses. The profound truth that this novelistic American universe bears witness to is that nothing in man belongs to him. Con- sidered in himself, man *is* not; he is nothing but a cluster of physiological or social determinants. Whether Dos Passos's characters succeed or fail, are happy or unhappy, satisfied or unfulfilled, the reason is never within themselves: it is due neither to their force of character nor their skill nor their wisdom. Dos Passos succeeds in showing us as fortuitous, adventitious, and external even those determinants generally considered to be intrinsic, situated in the deepest part of one's being—as for example Dick Ellsworth Savage's intelligence, Eveline Hutchins's charm, J. Ward Moorehouse's sex appeal, Margo Dowling's glamour, Glenn Spotswood's persuasive eloquence.[11] J. Ward Moorehouse's attractiveness to women is reduced to his blue eyes and his ingenuous manner; Glenn's ability to persuade and influence, to his heredity as son of a minister.

Dos Passos's characters are always borne along by some kind of determinism, generally economic. They represent in almost the pure state Spinoza's *esse in alienum*, as modified by Marx (or, even better, by Veblen). All their reality is outside them; consequently (although almost incidentally), the portrait of these beings without inner consistency consti- tutes the best indictment one can pronounce against the soci- ety that has produced—almost secreted—them; that has given them the false semblance of separate existence, the illusory

---

[11] In *Adventures of a Young Man*, a later Dos Passos novel.

prestige of individuality, without being able to lead them to true *being*. The portrayal of superficial, two-dimensional beings reduced to their most intrinsic determinants is already in itself a satire, an accusation against the established order, even if the social aims remain unformulated (and in *U.S.A.* they are actually quite clearly expressed, though in the most objective way, through certain newspaper quotes).[12]

The hidden ambiguity of Dos Passos's work derives from the possibility that the revolt against society is perhaps only the mask—as in Malraux and so many others—for a more profound metaphysical revolt. Beyond the social order, it is the Order of Things that he aims at and hits—and beyond that, a responsible Creator whom he does not at all believe in and whom, given his profound materialism, he is undoubtedly even unable to conceive of. This is responsible for the close-mouthed taciturnity of his books, in which the author can never speak in his own voice, in which he can only formulate—under the guise of the most anonymous,[13] impersonal, objective monologue possible—an accusation he knows (or believes) in advance to be condemned to fall in vain under an empty and echoless sky. From Dos Passos's work rises a mute protest, not only (as he probably believes) against capitalism but against the human condition, against the world-as-it-is, against, finally, the nature of Being. And if metaphysics is defined as an attempt to justify—or to impugn —Being, it can be seen that the very technique of *U.S.A.* is, like every good technique—according to Sartre's profound observation—pregnant with an entire metaphysic.

---

[12] One good example, too long to quote, ends Newsreel LXV.

[13] For example, the impassioned protest against the condemnation of Sacco and Vanzetti, the first few lines of which are quoted at the beginning of this chapter.

6 *Time in Dos Passos*

The special technique of *The Big Money* encompasses an entire, implicit metaphysic—the challenge of Being. It is important for another reason, too: thanks to this technique, Dos Passos's trilogy has a temporal structure. The several individual stories composing the trilogy, which are what one is first aware of, are not only different shots of a single reality but moments within a single development. This single development transcends each of them and exists only by virtue of the complex design they all form. It is possible to put them end to end and demonstrate their continuity; the occasional use of flashbacks when the author wants to present the past of a newly introduced character is no more frequent than it is in the movies. The nonnovelistic elements that frame the stories—the Newsreels, the Camera Eyes, the lyrical biographies—are thus seen to have a very important "linking" function: they assure the cosmic as well as the psychological continuity of the narrative. Because of them, the impersonal reality that is the subject of the book—the year 1919 or the economic inflation of the twenties—can unfold without interruption, independent of the individual consciousnesses in which it is embodied, and preserve the mythic quality Dos Passos wanted to achieve. They are like movie background music, which nobody listens to but everybody hears, and which prepares our subconscious for the images to come.

The Newsreels in particular have taken on the major role of the narrative—to measure the rhythm of time, to give us the uninterrupted sound that the film of life makes as it unrolls and winds off the reel behind the scenes. The Newsreels give us the unfolding world events that will have repercussions on the individual destinies of the characters. For example, J. Ward Moorehouse's story before and after his second marriage is cut in two not so much because of the marriage itself—which in no way interrupts a personal, emotional, and professional continuity—but because war is declared in Europe during his honeymoon. The war does not affect the characters' lives immediately, but it is destined to do so soon. Consequently, just as in Wagner's *Tristan and Isolde* the theme of Isolde's death is announced by a drum in the prelude long before it is taken up officially by the entire orchestra, so the "theme of war" is first presented longitudinally in the nonnovelistic elements of the book: a Newsreel filled with such headlines as "CZAR LOSES PATIENCE WITH AUSTRIA," "GENERAL WAR NEAR," "ASSASSIN SLAYS DEPUTY JUARES"; a biography of "Andrew Carnegie, Prince of Peace"; and a Camera Eye that appears to be the interior monologue of an English sailor. Then the narrative resumes. Further on, America's entry into the war is announced through a Camera Eye—the interior monologue of a couple (or a group) of New York leftist intellectuals—and a Newsreel punctuated by the refrain "It's a long way to Tipperary" and including headlines like "JOFFRE ASKS TROOPS NOW."

Similarly, in *The Big Money*, the biography of Rudolph Valentino—symbol of the handsome young man who has made it, of the gigolo elevated by the movies to the stature of a myth that has become a reality in the collective consciousness—is interpolated into the story at the moment when Margo Dowling leaves for Cuba with her gigolo husband. The biography itself is introduced by the last news item in the preceding Newsreel: "Rudolph Valentino, noted screen star, collapsed suddenly yesterday in his apartment at the Hotel Ambassador. Several hours later he underwent . . . " At this moment, just as on the radio, the voice suddenly changes and a new speaker "fades in" by announcing, in a completely different tone: "Adagio Dancer, The nineteenyearold son of a veterinary in Castellaneta . . . " And during all this time the story of Margo (and through her of an entire epoch) is going on uninterruptedly, though because of the novel's aesthetic we are only able to apprehend fragments of it.

Then a parenthesis begins—the story of Charley Anderson—followed by a new Newsreel and then by a Camera Eye that is the collective monologue of emigrants leaving for Havana, which brings us back to Margo's story. When Charley leaves for Detroit, where he will join a big airplane company and marry—in other words, where he will begin the series of adventures that will lead him to success, to his meeting with Margo, then to ruin and land speculations in Miami—we get a biography of the Wright brothers, aviation pioneers; a verse of "Valencia" and other songs evoking the charm of the South; a fragment of a speech by someone who has made a fortune in Miami; an excerpt from a brochure about installment buying; and so forth. The major events of Charley's life are prefigured in the evolution of society as a whole, which makes these events possible and determines their nature. His destiny is so little of his own making that it can be foretold and prophesied. Dos Passos's characters do not have their own inner rhythm; its place is taken by the objective, mechanical rhythm of social facts, which replace at every moment the personal time, the "lived time," that Charley, Margo, and Mary

French are incapable of possessing. It is social time, external time, that will carry them along in its inexorable unfolding.

One can now begin to see the profound connection at the heart of *U.S.A.* between the narrative technique of the stories and the objective elements that frame them. It is *necessary* that Dos Passos's characters have no positive inner existence, that they are not in the least masters of their fate, that they be equally incapable of controlling what happens to them and how they feel about it, that they marry for who knows what reason (Charley's marriage to Gladys and Margo's to Tony are from this point of view symbolic), and that they succeed or fail depending only upon whether they are being carried forward by the tide or left abandoned by it. And all of this is true even when, like Mary French, they *want* to give their lives a sense or meaning—by, for example, social action or self-sacrifice. Two of Dos Passos's later novels, *Adventures of a Young Man* and *Number One*, present us with a diptych of two equally absurd fates—that of Glenn Spotswood, martyr to the cause of the proletariat, and that of his brother Tyler, opportunist and dipsomaniac, the yes-man and tool of Chuck Crawford, the despicable boss of a Southern state, until Crawford decides to abandon him.

In modern society neither self-sacrifice nor ambition permits a man to be "captain of his soul, master of his fate," as the Victorian poets like Kipling or Henley had too naïvely hoped. And if Dos Passos has chosen to recount his characters' lives in that terrible preterit that *deadens* events as soon as they are so described to us; if he gives us their feelings and their states of consciousness by means of a third-person pseudo-inner monologue filled with clichés, adulterants that almost invariably come from a too-obvious hypocrisy, lacking every kind of reaction normal to an authentic and spontaneous life except for the lowest biological responses; if, thanks to the diabolic magic of his style, he thus pares modern man down to the bone to show him in his misery, his nakedness, his basic nothingness; if he does all these things, it is to prepare for the appearance, the display, the *epiphaneia*, of the major character of his book—Time: the inexorable and monstrous time of contemporary capitalist society as it incoherently unwinds in Newsreels; the time that elevates and casts down Margo, Charley, and Mary, with neither discernment nor justice, and rules over the empty consciousnesses it invades and tyrannizes.

"Time," says Schelling somewhere, "is the bad conscience of all barren metaphysics." It would not be at all arbitrary (or at least no more than it is to set forth any proposition) to begin to formulate an aesthetic of the novel by saying that Time is the main character of the novel; that the novel is the literary genre on which has devolved the task of exploring and explicating every aspect and every dimension of Time; and that the novel's current popularity and triumph is quite likely at least partly due to the unhappiness of the modern consciousness, one that has fallen away from its relationship with eternity—which it had successfully retained until the Renaissance—and is now wounded by a traumatism of Time, the presence of which is felt in most of the great contemporary novels from Faulkner to Virginia Woolf. One of the functions of criticism would then be to bring this to light and analyze it, to expose the wound if a thoroughgoing cure is shown to be impossible.

Within a dialectic of Time, the short story corresponds to the instant. An essentially impressionistic genre, it is—from Mérimée to Katherine Anne Porter and from the calm garden of Balzac's *Secrets de la Princesse de Cadignan* (*A Princess's Secrets*) to those short stories of Faulkner through which a tumultuous storm sweeps—an incision at a specific instant. To the novel, on the other hand, belongs the third dimension—

the opaque density of duration that is alone capable of inte-grating the two other dimensions. Obviously, this does not mean that the author has to show a character grow from birth to old age: the objective duration of the events he relates does not have to exceed the twenty-four hours of classical tragedy. Joyce's *Ulysses* and Virginia Woolf's *Mrs. Dalloway* are unquestionably the most famous (and the most deliberate) examples; a less well-known one is Louis Guilloux's *Le Sang noir*. And, of course, there is also Sterne's *Tristram Shandy*, which only manages to cover the first three days of the hero's life in its several hundred pages. But no one will be misled by appearances. The true time of the novel, its normal time, the time most often encountered (the very function of the genre seems to be to exploit it literarily), is what Bergson, in one of those simple and superficial views so characteristic of him, called "lived time." One senses this "lived time" in George Eliot's *Mill on the Floss*, in Balzac, in Meredith (to say nothing of in Rosamund Lehmann). And this "lived time" is what is lacking in Zola (but not in the Maupassant of *Une Vie*), and so ostentatiously present in Proust.

What makes Dos Passos stand out from other novelists is undoubtedly that the characteristic time of his novels does not, to the slightest degree, have this organic rhythm, the dense continuity of living tissue. His characters move within "dead time"—or rather "deadened time"—with neither spurts nor continuity, where each instant comes to the fore only to be immediately replunged into nothingness. An atomic time, like that of a Cartesian universe no longer at every instant supported by continuous creation, God having defaulted once and for all. But the discontinuity is only in the detail, in the psychological awareness of the characters. If the five hundred pages of *The Big Money* are read without interruption, the reader, far from having an impression of perpetual rupture, of atomism (which would seem the inevitable result of the purposeful dislocation of the story and its multiplicity of perspectives), feels rather as if he is being carried along by a swift current. This is because the psychological time within which the characters' states of consciousness, and their acts, unfold—and the essence of which is fragmentation—is not Dos Passos's real or basic time.

His true time is the time of Society—objective, inexorable, and spatialized. The hidden mainspring of *U.S.A.* is this implacable and regular machine rhythm, already evident in *Manhattan Transfer.* The powerful impetus that carries us through these three volumes for 1500 pages is the thumping of the locomotive, the regular "chug-chug" of a ship's boilers, the whir of a taxi motor in front of a building, or the relentless circuits of those moving headlines around the big newspaper buildings—their hallucinating monotony hypnotizing the crowd, causing the stock market crash, and provoking a rash of Wall Street suicides whose repercussions would eventually reach the Scandinavian farmers of Minnesota and the plantation population of South Carolina. The inexorable pulsation at the heart of Dos Passos's work is that of the basic, regular rhythm of the transmission belt in the heart of a factory—invisible, omnipresent, all-powerful. The rhythm of the modern world itself.

It is now possible to understand its implacability, its indifference, its unpredictability—greater by far than that of classical fatality (Dike, Themis, Ananke, and Moira), which the Greeks dared not call by one name and of which it is the contemporary form. Incapable of being accelerated or slowed down by men's will or their technique (which can influence everything but Time and which is the master only of details), Time obeys its own laws, which are known to no one else— not bankers, industrialists, or capitalists (especially not capitalists); not statesmen or economists; not Ford, Insull, Hearst (especially not Hearst), or Veblen, the old man with the heavy walk who "reels off, in a buzzing hum of sarcastic and subtle phrases, the logical and ineluctable rope of daily facts with which society will hang itself." It is what defeats Insull, by means of the bankers; Ford, by means of the economic depression and the failure of the installment-buying system; Valentino, by means of a sudden and mysterious gastritis. It is the mechanical divinity—implacable as only gears can be— that pulverizes individual destinies as soon as they slow down or speed up, as soon as the individual's rhythm is no longer in accord with the regular beat, inflexible as Fate, which is Time's own rhythm.

In this sense, the most typical evolution is that of Charley Anderson, whose life rhythm speeds up—with drink, women, the excitement of business, the exhilaration of speed, money, and success—to the point where he "goes faster than the music." It is as if he has received from Time an impulse so strong that it unhinges him, makes him speculate too daringly, drink too much, and lose his money until he arrives at the final, deeply symbolic catastrophe,[1] when, while driving his car at top speed while drunk, he is crushed by the train he has tried to pass. One cannot win a race against time any more than against light.

With this vision of Time as the monstrous divinity ensconced at the heart of the modern world, we have reached the very center of Dos Passos's work. Because of its outward diversity, this work seems, at first, to be iridescent and sparkling, but like every great work, it is essentially monotonous and almost obsessional. The inexorable fate that crushes John Andrews in *The Three Soldiers*; that, in *Manhattan Transfer*, causes Stan Emery to die a miserable death, Jimmy Herf to

---

[1] Actually, all fates in Dos Passos are symbolic. Another example is the fate of the errant sailor Joe Williams, tossed about from cargo to cargo, like the Flying Dutchman, throughout the entire war.

slowly disintegrate, and Ellen Oglethorpe to take refuge in a rich marriage; that has Glenn Spotswood taken prisoner by Spanish Loyalists in *Adventures of a Young Man* and that crushes his brother Tyler—this fate is always the same goddess in different disguises, the same one that alternately exalts and casts down the characters of *U.S.A.*, that turns the cameras with the toc-toc of a coffee grinder or a machinegun, that sweeps Woodrow Wilson, Fred Taylor, and Isadora Duncan toward their varied and futile destinies.

Here we touch upon the central intuition at the heart of every profoundly original work, an intuition that the writer has had to use every resource of his art, every bit of his life itself, to communicate to us. The compensation for our attentive reading, abstract reflection, and critical meditation is the abrupt, direct, and incandescent apprehension that suddenly brings us face to face with what Henry James called "the figure in the carpet"—the profound and yet obvious secret that the artist (and this is both his servitude and his grandeur) was not able to give us except through the chaotic procession of numerous, sensually apprehendable appearances that constitute the texture of his work.

This is the justification for the outward complexity of Dos Passos's trilogy, a work that runs the risk of disconcerting, if not actually rebuffing, the reader. The author most certainly could not have communicated his intuition of an implacable, mechanistic, and socialized Time that is the sole regulator of the world by means of a simple narrative about the lives of his characters. He had to illumine them, clarifying the orientation (without which they would simply have appeared as chaotic) by framing them with objective elements, historic landmarks, dates as impersonal as those on a calendar, taken from exactly the same web of external and indifferent time within which individual destinies are unwinding. Regardless of how strange it may seem at first reading, the technique used by the author of *U.S.A.* is no more the byzantine refinement of a writer eager to proclaim his originality and somehow attract the attention of a blasé public than was that of Joyce in *Ulysses* or the deliberately obscure narration of Faulkner. It was without doubt the only means by which he could achieve his end.

One question remains: Is Dos Passos's desired effect immediately and truly achieved through these formal innovations to which he had recourse, or is the significance of his work only discerned after critical analysis? In other words, is the technique of *U.S.A.* important because of its immediate efficacy, or will it pass into literary history as an artistic curiosity, an unsuccessful example—instructive by its very failure —of what human ambition and ingenuity have aimed at?

Here the critic must invoke his personal experience and become just another reader. I thus confess to having long ignored the nonnovelistic elements (and their ultimate significance) of the first two volumes of *U.S.A.* except for a few of the biographies; to having deliberately skipped over them to get on with the story; to having frequently been annoyed by them, especially by the Camera Eyes and the Newsreels, which upset me just as the bits of newspapers the surrealists integrated into their collages did; and even to having sometimes treated *1919* as I was later to treat *Les Hommes de bonne volonté*, foraging through the volumes, like a child picking all the raisins out of the pudding, for the adventures of the characters I liked best—well punished, to be sure, when I realized that important things had happened to those preferred characters in the course of one of the sections I had skipped.

From rereading to rereading, I made additional efforts to apprehend, to integrate into my vision of the whole, those pages I had at first skipped. But the decisive step was taken only when I received the long-awaited copy of *The Big*

Money. Though I was at first disappointed not to find the names of any of the beloved characters of the first two volumes in the table of contents of this third, I was able, for the first time and without effort, to read the book from beginning to end, as the author would have wanted it to be read. (It is unquestionably a good thing that novelists, especially those whose technique is ambitious, are unaware of the bad habits of even their most impassioned and most conscientious readers.) For the first time, I not only did not skip, but felt from the beginning the *connections* between the stories as well as their novelistic continuity—perceiving immediately, for example, the subtle counterpoint formed by the newspaper headlines, the camera monologue, and the biographies of Ford, Hearst, and Valentino that surround the "solos" of Charley, Margo, and Mary French. Dos Passos's technique was finally proved efficacious.

An adaptation this complete to a technique so initially upsetting obviously presupposes a long familiarity with the work. But many writers would subscribe to Gide's declaration that he no longer writes except to be "reread" and would agree with him that they can only hope to win their case by "appeal." In addition, it can be said without paradox that the novel is the genre that most requires time in which to deliver up to us all its marrow, and that true comprehension of such a work begins only when the first superficial pleasure of reading, the elementary delight we all find in following a story, is over. The true reader of novels, the one every novelist worthy of the name should have, is not the man whose tastes are the most varied and whose culture is the most extensive but the one who tirelessly reads and rereads a small number of select works—Dickens, Meredith, or Balzac; *War and Peace, La Chartreuse de Parme,* or *À la Recherche du temps perdu*. One may advise such a reader, if he wishes from time to time to enrich his universe, to add to his list Bernanos,

Graham Greene, or Dos Passos, even if the unraveling of these texts, the breaking into new territory, demands of him some small initial effort.

The reading of Dos Passos will compensate him not only by peopling the domains of his imagination with new creations but by refining and making more subtle his novelistic perception. His inner breadth, his receptivity to a certain literary polyphony, will be considerably augmented by the assimilation of a book like *The Big Money*. And though this quasi-gymnastic function of enlargement, of the modification of human awareness, is not the essential mission of art, it is not unimportant. The daring of first the impressionists and then the cubists gradually trained the public's eye, teaching it to apprehend immediately the beauty and meaning of pictures that fifty years earlier would have been considered unintelligible and scandalous chaos. The extent of man's plasticity is so undefined that there is almost an obligation for the writer to take advantage of the possibilities of the human spirit in order to transform systematically the novelistic vision of his contemporaries. (There is an analogous obligation for the painter, the filmmaker, the composer.) Joyce and Dos Passos, who were pioneers in this literary reeducation, understood this and thus predisposed readers to future works that will be even more subtle and complex than their own. More than for the specific contribution of their researches into the technique of the novel (for it is hard to see how a technique as personal and as closely adapted to the unique message of *U.S.A.* can be imitated), these authors deserve the thanks of future novelists for having prepared their public. Because of their efforts, the impersonal novel will perhaps some day be possible.

From this point of view, it is curious to note that the technique of Dos Passos's two later books, *Adventures of a*

Young Man and *Number One*, marks, in relation to that of *The Big Money*, a sort of regression, a return to the traditional, individualistic form of the novel, centered on one character cut off from the elements that would integrate him with impersonal history. It is no less strange to note that the author of *Manhattan Transfer* underwent a gradual detachment from the novelistic genre. After he wrote *The Ground We Stand On* and a sociological study (remarkable, to be sure), *State of the Nation*, he wrote a life of Jefferson, a typically American hero. The reasons for this must be sought in the impasse to which a conception of the world such as his—one full of implicit contradictions, making for both the grandeur and the limitations of his work—must lead.

The specifically literary merits of Dos Passos are a perfect objectivity in the presentation of the facts, which he shares with many another American novelist of his generation, and a sort of untamed energy that he brings even to the portrayal of despair—an energy linked to a profound vitality that is also very American. What gives the best pages of *The Big Money* such an inimitable voice, what gives such value to the biographies of Hearst and Veblen, to the funeral oration of Sacco and Vanzetti, to the portrait of the vagabond that closes the book, is the union (which only Dos Passos was able to make work) of an extremely vehement tone with absolute impartiality. It is remarkable, for example, that nowhere in the biography of Hearst does he use his own voice to cast aspersions or to stigmatize; and yet we feel the vibration of his indignation, both passionate and contained, in every one of his sentences. This indictment by Dos Passos is not even primarily based on Hearst's specific or particular acts, but rather on his basic deficiency: more than the adversary of the League of Nations or the man responsible for Manila Bay, Hearst is the spoiled little boy who thinks himself Caesar and is not even Alcibiades, the man who never managed "to bridge the tiny Rubicon between amateur and professional politics," the man whose verdict will have to be the indifferent handful of earth thrown on his grave in the last two lines of his biography. Here lies "a spent Caesar grown old with spending—never man enough to cross the Rubicon."

Dos Passos can condemn, can *damn*, just by showing people as they are, by describing them faithfully, by drawing their outlines with an exactitude more implacable than could be achieved through any extravagance of tone. The note most indicative of his work, that which makes it unique, is this objective indignation. This is because his indignation goes beyond the individual to attack the whole system that has produced him—and not only, as orthodox Marxists are simple enough to believe, the capitalist system. Dos Passos's anger cannot help but be objective because it is directed ultimately against Being itself.

Thus, Samuel Insull, destroyed by the bankers and dragging the stockholders of his eighty-five companies into ruin with him, is by no means a vile scoundrel—or even a crooked financier or a dishonest director. He did nothing more than understand and exploit the truth formulated by Barnum in the celebrated phrase, "There's a sucker born every minute." Then he became the victim of the fragility of the capitalist system. He is not, as a man, hateful; he has only been the instrument of the order of things. The novelist does not have to judge his characters: he has neither the need nor the right to do so. The criticism of people and institutions will automatically take place in the mind of the reader, provided they are presented with truth and vigor. Dos Passos's art is the more convincing for its perfect objectivity.

But even this merit entails its opposite. If Dos Passos, conforming to the evangelical precept, thus abstains from any judgments, it is because he is fundamentally incapable of judging, for judgment presupposes an organized system of positive norms, of firm and cohesive certainties in whose name one can render a verdict. Dos Passos's message is as deliberately, as passionately, negative as Socrates's. Like Veblen, his favorite hero, he is congenitally incapable of an unambiguous "yes." It is quite clear, despite the apparent impartiality of his narration, that his political sympathies in *U.S.A.* go to all those who, like Eugene Debs and Thorstein Veblen, have been vanquished because they said "no!"—to dissidents of all types, to the Spanish anarchists, to the revolutionary Mexicans (among whom Mac, the only character in *U.S.A.* to find happiness, will go to live), to the members of the IWW, to those whose actions will probably never even get into the history books. His heroes are always heretics, like Glenn Spotswood or Ben Compton, excluded from the party for which they have sacrificed themselves, broken in body and spirit, having lost even the belief in the efficacy of their fight and their martyrdom, but keeping to the end that critical spirit affirmed by Glenn Spotswood's intellectual testament, written from the prison in which he was put by the Republicans: "I, Glenn Spotswood, being of sound mind and emprisoned body, do bequeath to the international working class my hope of a better world." It is significant that when Dos Passos (referring to the architect Frank Lloyd Wright) wants to make a list of the fundamental needs of man, he finds (like an Epicurean listing authentic pleasures) that only negative suggestions occur to him:

> (Tell us, doctors of philosophy, what are the needs of a man. At least a man needs to be notjailed notafraid nothungry notcold not without love, not a worker for a power he has never seen that cares nothing for the uses and needs of a man or a woman or a child.)[2]

[2] John Dos Passos, *1919*, Boston, Houghton Mifflin, 1946, p. 504. —Tr.

It is easy to see why he does not express his anger in intellectual terms: he cannot. Indeed, it is hard to see in the name of what, by virtue of which doctrine, he *could* get angry. Veblen did not get angry either. At most, he allowed himself some occasional irony; in general, he merely set before his audience the contradictions of the system. Like him, throughout *U.S.A.* Dos Passos weaves the "logical inescapable rope of matter of fact for a society to hang itself by." He does not have to condemn his characters; they will destroy themselves on their own. There is nothing constructive, nothing positive, nothing affirmative, in his work, and in this way he escapes both the aridity of the thesis novel and the naïveté of the writer-saviors, who insist on propounding remedies against the incurable ill that is man's existence. He is all but forced to remain faithful to the great mission of literature, which is only to *show* reality, not to improve it.

At the same time, because of this profound negativism, his books will always seem somewhat lacking, almost incomplete. His protest goes much beyond political protest: he is quite obviously suspicious of all collectivities, all forms of society, of no matter what kind. Would Veblen really have been more at home in a communist regime? And Socrates? It is not a religious protest, either, given Dos Passos's deep-rooted and almost unconscious materialism (obvious, for example, in the enumeration of the fundamental human needs cited above); nor is it, given his extremely concrete nature, a metaphysical one, except implicitly. Ultimately, it is not easy to see clearly exactly what he is angry about; he is just angry, that is all. Very simply, he says *no*. If nothing were known of him but what comes through from his writing, it would be very easy to see the author of *The Big Money* as another Veblen—an old bear, stubborn and taciturn, that has ended up speaking only in growls:

Veblen
asked too many questions, suffered from a constitutional inability to say yes.
Socrates asked questions, drank down the bitter drink one night when the first cock crowed,
but Veblen
drank it in little sips through a long life . . .[3]

But we know that Dos Passos, fortunately, did not drain the chalice to the dregs, at least not as Socrates or even Veblen did. What saves him from complete nihilism is undoubtedly his prodigious vitality, the extraordinary vigor that he cannot help but bring even to a message as passionately negative as his own. His denials are as positive, as energetic, as most people's affirmations. His books "end badly" in every conceivable way, and yet we are not depressed by reading them. At the end of *The Big Money* Charley Anderson is killed in a car accident; J. W. Moorehouse is growing old alone and embittered; Dick Savage, rotten at the core, like an overripe fruit, outlives himself, seeking a refuge in alcohol from the sense of the futility of his existence; Margo Dowling will certainly not be as great a star in sound films as she had been in the silents; and Eveline Hutchins commits suicide with an overdose of barbiturates.

The historical destinies are no more comforting: Isidora Duncan and Rudolph Valentino die tragically; Frank Lloyd Wright is the "patriarch of the new building/not without honor except in his own country"; Fred Taylor, the mystic of efficiency, dies in a fit of depression without having seen the fruition of his American Plan; Ford, stupidity itself, "the crackerbarrel philosopher," who has known only how to exploit the system until the moment when the system turns against him, grows old barricaded on the family farm, pro-

[3] John Dos Passos, *The Big Money*, Boston, Houghton Mifflin, 1946, p. 107.—Tr.

tected by an army of detectives and trembling with fear before the new America he has helped create, that of the strikers and the starving. Good or bad, egotistical or selfless, for capitalism—like Charley, Margo, and Tyler Spotswood—or against it—like Mary French, Glenn Spotswood, and Ben Compton—Dos Passos's characters are destined to failure, to death, or to an absurd martyrdom like Glenn's.

D. H. Lawrence, who loved the unflinching honesty of *Manhattan Transfer*, described it as "a great ravel of flights from nothing to nothing." This definition could quite accurately be applied to *U.S.A.*, which opens with a prologue entitled "Vag," in which we see a young man walking avidly among the nocturnal crowds of a big city, watching, listening, eager to grasp life with both hands—and which closes with an epilogue also entitled "Vag," in which a young man (and why not the same one?) is vainly waiting along the side of a highway, having realized none of his desires, having achieved nothing. For Dos Passos, the structure of the world in which we live is composed of what Jaspers calls the "cipher of failure," and it is this objective hieroglyph that he makes us see—like a watermark—on each page of his books.

Once these three volumes of *U.S.A.*, the apogee of failure and despair, were written—and with all desirable impartiality and rigor—it is not very clear what there remained for the author to do. In them he attained that point of perfection in the work of a writer where every merit becomes inseparable from a limitation. Since his two later novels do not in any sense constitute a renewal of his universe—not even an appreciable enrichment of it—I have in a sense spoken of them as if they were supplements to the trilogy that remains his masterpiece. The most curious thing about them is that they are a return to a narrative focused on an individual, which is rather astonishing on the part of a writer who had so deliberately set himself the task of creating an impersonal novel. But this is because Dos Passos (and Hemingway too, despite *For Whom the Bell Tolls*) always remained an impenitent individualist. As Orestes Brown noted, the reformation of the masses cannot be accomplished unless one first reforms the component individuals. In the final analysis, the only positive virtues Dos Passos puts any hope in are the strictly individual ones: he believes in a kind of artist's morality, difficult to make general, that consists of absolute honesty and rectitude of vision—the effort to arrive at the same implacable objectivity as the camera.

One can hardly suppose that Dos Passos was happy with his literary position. When Veblen's wife finally left him, he wrote to one of his friends: "The President doesn't approve of my domestic arrangements: nor do I." That "nor do I" is undoubtedly the only commentary that his position as artist will allow an aware and critical person like Dos Passos to make. His efforts to renew himself by means of sociological studies, biographies of Jefferson, etc., must be seen as the equivalent of the growls of a taciturn bear, which is how Veblen, at the end of his life, was reduced to communicating with his fellow men. When the novelistic idiom stutters, becomes disjointed, it is called reportage.

It is also difficult to believe that Dos Passos will manage to maintain his equilibrium, as he grows older, on the level of "happy-in-spite-of-all-despair" that he managed to reach in *U.S.A.*, even in its artistic expression. The "lion-become-old" will probably not be able to preserve the personal union, perhaps unique in literature, of the three antagonistic elements of nihilism, objectivity, and emotional violence. Judging from his latest works, it is not very likely that the unballasting will take place at the expense of impartiality and that he will cede to the temptation of a hopeless but vehement lyricism like that of Henry Miller, that American of Paris. It seems equally unlikely that his vision will acquire an optimism that could only be achieved at the expense of lucidity. What he most risks losing is the vital buoyancy (very "war-correspondent") that makes it possible to walk serenely between two abysses whose depths are quite clearly seen, and then to describe very objectively what has been measured. His work will thus perhaps continue to evolve in the direction of the "document" —impartial rather than gripping. With Dos Passos, the novel will have made itself so impersonal that it will no longer be fiction, a work of imagination perhaps capable (who knows?) of transforming the world.

7 *Hemingway, or the Exaltation of the Moment*

For some time now Hemingway's publishers have marketed him not as the author of *A Farewell to Arms* but as the author of *For Whom the Bell Tolls*. The first of these books—the only truly successful "war novel" America has given us—was for many of us an immediate and probably too perfect demonstration of what he was capable of. We found the same talent in *The Sun Also Rises* and in his short stories, but less complete and less perfect.

Both Dos Passos and Faulkner failed in their attempts to exorcise their war experiences (the former with *Three Soldiers*, the latter with *Soldiers' Pay*—two tortuous books in which these experiences were insufficiently distilled) because they were straining toward new works, which were this time, as if liberated by the failure of the earlier books, fully to succeed. On the other hand, it seemed as though Hemingway was destined to remain prisoner of a too well-balanced first novel; even its good points worked against him. The discretion; the deliberately elliptical quality so characteristic of his style that each time an understating author like Camus or Mouloudji appears in France there is sure to be a critic who will say of his work "It's Hemingwayesque"; the restraint with which he pictured even brutality—all these negative merits, no matter how precious they might have been, ended by depriving his stories of the depth, of the human significance, without which there is no great art. Too stripped, too objective, too brief also (and I am not referring to their physical dimensions), his stories seemed somewhat skimpy; more and more they were reduced to the level of simple reportages, a purely stenographic record of what was there. Leafing through the collection issued in France as *Ten Indians*, which includes stories written at various times and printed without regard to chronological order, one is struck by their extreme unevenness. Most of them—and especially the earliest of them—are superficial and linear.

The "two-dimensional" nature of his art—of which Hemingway was surely quite aware—undoubtedly explains the special technique of a book like *In Our Time*, a collection of stories that are all concerned with peacetime but are inserted into a kind of continuous narrative relating the wartime impressions of someone very like the hero of *A Farewell to Arms*—indeed, like the author himself. It is as though the author, by this artifice (as well as by the collection of these stories in one volume and their resultant convergence), had tried to confer on them the depth and the density that none of them possessed on its own if considered apart from the others. A similar thinness characterizes "The Light of the World," a story Hemingway once acknowledged as one of his favorites—and one that he alone has liked. His artistic realization was probably not up to his intentions, so he was not able to endow the story with the human richness and meaning necessary to communicate to the reader the transcendent significance, the special dimension, it had for him.

Prisoner of an art that had almost immediately reached its point of maximum perfection, incapable of integrating into this too-perfect form the later acquisitions of an experience he had perhaps not quite assimilated, Hemingway seemed one of the most noteworthy victims of that well-known fatality which seems to want American novelists to die young—either literally, as in the case of F. Scott Fitzgerald or Nathanael West, or metaphorically, as with William Saroyan or John O'Hara, two victims of success and Hollywood.

The apparent serenity of *A Farewell to Arms* was completely superficial. The objective quality of the narration does not bear witness to true maturity—that of a man who can speak impartially of his suffering because he has overcome it —but rather evokes the anesthetized indifference of the wounded man who (as happens to Henry in *A Farewell to Arms*) is traumatized by the psychological shock he has received and does not yet feel the pain of his wounds. The author's attitude (difficult to differentiate from that of his character) was basically not a viable one: it was impossible to prolong indefinitely such a taciturn refusal to act, to continue calmly to say "no" to the war and to the world without explanation or indignation, to maintain to the end the same stubborn noncooperation with existence. There is something fundamentally adolescent about *A Farewell to Arms*. Without the aesthetic power of its expression, without Hemingway's sharp sensibility and human richness, its stance would be tiresomely like that of the spoiled child who does not want to play any more in a world where everyone cheats.

This "adolescent prodigy" aspect explains the kind of stagnation evidenced in Hemingway's art after its brilliant beginnings. He very quickly became a prisoner of his legend; he could not escape from the world he had prematurely created for himself. *The Sun Also Rises* had given us the same kind of hero as *A Farewell to Arms*, but he is even more nihilistic—very representative of the post-World War I "lost generation": wildly individualistic, feeling perpetually threatened by society (as Wyndham Lewis so accurately observed, the Hemingway hero is someone "to whom something has been done"), believing in nothing, returning from everywhere almost without having been anywhere, refusing to sacrifice himself for *anything* that transcends human existence, and, finally, contenting himself perfectly with his lot (at least momentarily) and finding in wine, women, bullfighting, and big-game hunting sufficient sources of satisfaction, almost indefinitely renewable, for a man in good health.

Hemingway's particular merit was to have expressed this simple, brutal, and quite elementary (not to say puerile) conception of life with all the resources of a very subtle art—one that on the surface seemed simple and made no effort to attract attention. His debt to Gertrude Stein has often been noted (without, to my knowledge, ever having been analyzed precisely). He surely learned from her the spareness of style, the restrained vocabulary, the use of litotes, and most likely also the infinite rhythmic possibilities inherent in prose. Much later, in *Death in the Afternoon* (which is by no means a bullfighting manual), he notes the limits of a craft solely sprung from reporting, as his was:

> In writing for a newspaper, you told what happened, and with one trick or another, you communicated the emotion aided by the element of timeliness which gives a certain emotion to any account of something that has happened on that day. But the real thing, the sequence of motion and fact which made the emotion and which would be as valid in a year or ten years or, with luck and if you stated it purely enough, always, was beyond me and I was working very hard to get it.[1]

[1] Ernest Hemingway, *Death in the Afternoon*, London, Jonathan Cape, 1962, p. 10.—Tr.

What Hemingway was looking for was a prose that would be more complex than that of simple objective description and yet would keep all its purity. "I would like to see," he says a bit farther on, "just where prose could go if one could give it a fourth dimension, a fifth if necessary, something more difficult to write than poetry." He was looking for a prose that no one had ever written before, but one that could be done "without tricks or trickery of any kind, with nothing that can be corrupted by what comes after."

Perfect though it was, this art was nevertheless destined to seem elementary so long as its content remained so. For years Hemingway's dilemma could be ascribed to his using a very sophisticated technique to express an extremely simplistic vision of the world. The unsuccessful novel *To Have and Have Not* marks a crisis in his inner evolution as well as a turning point in his artistic career. The book was written eight years after *A Farewell to Arms*, under the influence of the 1929 economic crisis and its repercussions, at a time when the author, like so many other American writers, became aware of and preoccupied with social questions. Here, too, Hemingway was representative of his entire generation; the situation of Harry Morgan, the upright smuggler who is the hero of *To Have and Have Not*, has an exemplary value (as has that of the author) insofar as his situation is that of each of us (with different modalities).

Like Harry Morgan and like Hemingway, modern man finds himself cast adrift in a confused world that he finds frightening and vaguely scandalous. He tries to get along on his own for a while, like the hero of *A Farewell to Arms* during the retreat from Caporetto, but this individualism, no matter how passionate, is a dead end: it leads only to the almost Byronic nihilism of *The Sun Also Rises*. Hemingway's uneasiness about his own values is reflected in the novel

about Harry Morgan. Morgan is the typical Hemingway ad-
venturer, this time not by deliberate choice (like the hero of
A Farewell to Arms or even like Robert Jordan in *For Whom
the Bell Tolls*), but because of economic necessity: Morgan is
even more overwhelmed by society than were the heroes of
the earlier books. This upright man is forced to become a
smuggler and almost a pirate after having tried, for many
years, to earn his living legitimately by renting out his boat to
the idle rich who want to go fishing for marlin off Havana.
But he is finally overcome and dies the absurd death of the
solitary, of those who have not experienced the fraternity of
men and who lack the company of their peers to the very end.
This truly virile hero is beaten because he is alone, while all
around him the multifaceted and scandalous world that has
crushed him—the world where fishermen, Cuban terrorists,
millionaires, snobs, and parasites exist side by side—continues
its vain agitation.

The very texture of the book reproduces both the incoherence of this universe the author wishes to set before us
and the instability of his personal position. When *To Have
and Have Not* appeared in America in 1936, the critics were
especially disconcerted by its "gangster story" aspect. The
lack of a homogeneous technique and the confusion of the
episodes very faithfully reflect Hemingway's own inner crisis:
his profound disturbance at what he saw around him, his
unsentimental perception of the inadequacy of the individualism that had till then been his only ethic, his inability to find
anything worthwhile to substitute for it. The book as a whole
does not make sense except as a blind, choleric, passionate
protest against something that is not even clearly defined. We
are not sure, for example, if it is "capitalist society" or, more
generally, "the way things are" that Hemingway is rebelling
against. The same characteristics—the equivocal and disillusioned tone, the futile derision—are to be found in the short

stories written in Madrid at the same time as *To Have and Have Not*—in "Ten Indians," for example, or especially in "Today Is Friday," that bitter, ironic, ambiguous retelling of the Crucifixion by three soldiers who were there and who, that evening, sit in a cabaret drinking and talking about it.

On reading *For Whom the Bell Tolls*, we can measure what Hemingway gained in inner ripeness during this crisis (a crisis most great writers undergo at the beginning of their careers, but which he underwent fifteen years later). The finest praise of this book undoubtedly came from the English critic V. S. Pritchett, who declared that it was Hemingway's "most adult novel." One might go further and add that it was with this book that Hemingway first truly became an adult. For the first time he completely cut the umbilical cord between himself and his creation. He gives us in Robert Jordan a "detached" hero, so detached from the personal and finite in his own destiny that he would sooner accept death than feel himself separate, or pridefully cut off from, the rest of the world. In other words, he is a character capable of completely dedicating himself to a cause rather than one who refuses, as does the hero of *A Farewell to Arms*, to go on playing the game. Correlatively, Hemingway finally managed to write that "multidimensional" prose, swollen with meaning and inner richness, that he had never stopped dreaming of but had almost never achieved. He managed to write a *true* novel —in which the instant gets denser in duration—and not simply a long story (like *A Farewell to Arms*) or a collection of stories centered on the same hero (like *To Have and Have Not*).

Robert Jordan, the hero of *For Whom the Bell Tolls*, is, like Henry in *A Farewell to Arms* (whose older brother he might be), one of those Americans involved in conflicts they have no direct connection with. World War I found them fighting in the ranks of the Italian army, and the Spanish Civil

War saw them at the side of the Republicans. Jordan is given the job of destroying a bridge under impossibly dangerous conditions, just at the beginning of a big offensive. In the course of his mission he meets a young girl, Maria, and falls madly in love with her. After spending several extraordinary days together—days whose timeless intensity makes them the equivalent of the long years of peaceful life together they will never have—he blows up the bridge, is seriously wounded almost immediately afterward, and is left there to face certain death. That is all. He is not sure that the destruction of the bridge is of any use; the offensive it is supposed to support may not actually be a true offensive; in the end, it is not even certain that it has taken place. In any event, it is almost surely doomed to failure.

What is more, we know from the beginning—as Robert Jordan and all those with him know—that he will die in the course of the operation. It makes no difference to him: he has managed to attain complete disinterestedness, absolute selflessness. Even when he finds the love that gives his life immeasurable value and confers on it a significance he has never previously imagined, he persists in his sacrifice. Unlike the hero of *A Farewell to Arms,* who said after Caporetto "I am through," he refuses to prefer himself to the world, to choose himself and his personal life over the world. Regardless of the disappointments humanity has caused him, he does not consent to cut himself off from the community of mankind. Robert Jordan accepts the totality of reality such as it is; he willingly assumes solidarity with the world as a whole. In terms of the novel, this is the concrete explanation of his participation in a war that is not his own—a participation that neither his taste for adventure nor his sympathy for Spain nor even his militant and liberal background suffices to explain when that participation makes it necessary for him to give clear-sighted consent to his loss of self. This is also the meaning of John Donne's admirable epigraph, which gives the book both its title and its metaphysical atmosphere:

> No man is an Iland, intire of it selfe; every man is a peece of the continent, a part of the maine; if a Clod be washed away by the Sea, Europe is the lesse, as well as if a Promontorie were, as well as if a mannor of thy friends or of thine owne were; any mans death diminishes me, because I am involved in Mankinde; and therefore never send to know for whom the bell tolls: It tolls for thee.

No character in *For Whom the Bell Tolls* embodies the sullen attitude of Henry in *A Farewell to Arms*—always sure that he is right and the world wrong, always convinced that he has in some way been wronged. Not for one moment does Robert Jordan rebel: he is angered neither by the dullness or mediocrity of the men who help him nor by his vanity or the difficulty of his mission; he does not complain about having been flung into a universe in which planes are never where they should be to support the infantry, in which the flanks always crumble at the very moment when the central attack is finally about to succeed. On the contrary, all this seems to give him an extra reason for going on: "He had seen enough commanders to whom all orders were impossible. That swine Gomez in Estremadura. He had seen enough attacks when the flanks didn't advance because it was impossible. No, he would carry out the orders. . . . "[2]

He never considers abandoning the struggle; of all possible choices, that one seems the most chimerical. He has become aware that the tragic is a reality at the heart of all existence, and he has accepted this knowledge in the deepest part of his soul. Something like this attitude—*amor fati*, an active pessimism—could already be seen in *To Have and Have Not* (for example, in some admirable scenes between Harry

---

[2] Ernest Hemingway, *For Whom the Bell Tolls*, New York, Scribner's, 1940, p. 162.—Tr.

Morgan and his wife), but there it seems almost like the author's personal property. He had not yet managed to embody it fully and perfectly in his book, to create for it an "objective correlative"—to use Eliot's expression—that would exactly correspond to it; it was as though his craft had not kept pace with his inner evolution.

All the characters in *For Whom the Bell Tolls* share, though to a lesser degree, the hero's convictions. Even the most contemptible of them, the traitor Pablo, cannot carry his cowardice out to the end: he rejoins the partisans he had temporarily abandoned. "I was so alone," he says. There is an analogous moment in *A Farewell to Arms* when Henry, a semivoluntary deserter who has taken refuge in Stresa, feels closing in on him, for a moment, the solitude of the child who has played hookey from school and is thinking nostalgically of the work and play of his friends, from whom he is now cut off. But thanks to Catherine's love, which constructs a new universe around him, he bears up under this solitude, whereas Robert Jordan, even with Maria, would not be able to endure the isolation of a man cut off by his betrayal from the community of those who fight on.

And he is not the only one to feel this way. When he explains his mission, all of them—Pablo; his woman, Pilar; Augustin the Gypsy—understand, more or less quickly depending on their intelligence, that it means death for them all. And all of them, after having reacted according to their individual temperaments (Pilar by exploding emotionally, Pablo by temporarily giving in to his cowardice and running away, and so forth), end by resigning themselves to it. But they will be with Robert Jordan to the end, and from this springs their common grandeur: that of Anselmo, the old mountain guide who remains faithful to his post in the midst of a terrible snowstorm; that of Maria; that of Pilar, "the woman of loose morals," whose vocabulary is full of obscenity but who is possessed of deep wisdom—the most extraordinary figure in the book. Like Robert Jordan, like the heroes of Malraux or Saint-Exupéry, all the characters of *For Whom the Bell Tolls* are oriented toward—with greater or lesser perfection—the same attitude: an attitude one does not know whether to call heroism or charity, an attitude defined so well by Saint-Exupéry in *Pilote de guerre* (*Flight to Arras*), in describing his Hochedé, as "that state of permanent grace which surely is the final consummation of man."[3]

From a technical point of view, the book's major interest lies in its being a short story raised to the power of a novel. As is usual in stories, *For Whom the Bell Tolls* takes place within a very short time-span and describes a brief and violent act devoid of inner complexity. It revolves around a simple and almost linear plot—the destruction of the bridge. Yet into this brief act Hemingway manages to bring together his hero's entire life, the total extent of a civil war, and almost the complete reality of Spain—just as Robert Jordan must condense a whole life, an eternity of happiness and love, into the three nights he spends with Maria. In one of Hemingway's later stories, "The Snows of Kilimanjaro" (in my opinion one of his most perfect stories and one of those he himself prefers), there is an analogous attempt to encompass a life in a short narrative, but in twenty-five pages rather than the four hundred and fifty of *For Whom the Bell Tolls*. By using simple, almost classical methods, he is able without distending or distorting it to stuff novelistic *durée* into the eternal present which is the time of the short story.

In *For Whom the Bell Tolls*, Pablo, leader of the guerrilla group that is supposed to help Robert, has a woman, Pilar, and it is her stories that interrupt the action. These

---

[3] Antoine de Saint-Exupéry, *Flight to Arras*, trans. by Lewis Galantière, New York, Reynal & Hitchcock, 1942, p. 55.—Tr.

flashbacks give us the story of the first days of the Spanish Republic and make the book a kind of fresco of the revolution, the particular action of a given story being like a gap in the wall through which we can contemplate a large section of history. And it is an impartial fresco, too, one that does not spare us the story of the cruelties committed by the Republicans. We plunge even more deeply into the past: the matadors' banquet brings us back to before the proclamation of the Republic, to the time of Pilar's liaison with Finito, the tubercular matador who because of his small size was always wounded at the time of the kill. At other times Robert Jordan's interior monologue interrupts the narration and gives it its depth: we learn that he is a Spanish professor in Missoula, Montana, but that he has the military art in his blood because of his grandfather, who fought valiantly first against the Sioux and then in the Civil War. Then the snow begins to fall, delaying the operation and enveloping everything in its blanketing atmosphere (the snow plays an important role in the plot as well as in the poetic construction of the book). By means of all these techniques, not one of which was artificial, Hemingway was able to give—"without faking or cheating," as he had always wished—the three dimensions and the temporal density characteristic of the novel to an essentially linear story. At the same time, thanks to this novelistic density, he was able to express himself more fully and more completely in this book than in any of his previous works, in which the need to "write up something," to transcribe on paper the spectacle under his eyes, often carried the day against the desire to express himself and what was best in him.

Similar merits are to be found in two long stories that are among the best he has written: "The Short Happy Life of Francis Macomber" and "The Snows of Kilimanjaro." As I have said, the technique of the latter is similar to that of *For Whom the Bell Tolls*: the hero, who knows he is going to die, sees his life pass before him in a parade of images and physical sensations. Because he is also a novelist, he directs his life toward an imaginary future by dreaming of all the marvelous stories he will never write. In "Francis Macomber," the technique is even more simple, more stripped of all artifice: here Hemingway renounced the basically facile technique of flashbacks separated from the present-tense narration by means of italics, and the whole past relationship of Francis Macomber and his wife is evoked in miniature through the presentation of their present conflict.

It is neither accidental nor unimportant that these two stories, like *For Whom the Bell Tolls*, end with the death of the hero—or, as one is almost tempted to say, with the "moment of the kill." Hemingway's time is in essence a time without a future, amputated from this dimension that would normally allow him to project and extend himself. It is only as a game, and on the level of a sort of deliberately mythomaniac and compensatory dream, that Robert Jordan is able to imagine a future life with Maria in Madrid or in America: he does not *really* believe in it. And the hero of *A Farewell to Arms* also cannot envisage anything beyond his present life with Catherine. All these lives have their horizons closed beforehand; they would remain sealed even if they did not end tragically, and in one sense it could be said that the story's denouement has to be bloody because no other outcome is conceivable. This is what is responsible for the resultant impression of a calm—tacit, one might say—despair. Nothing Hemingway can do can make the future become truly alive, for him or for his characters; at best he succeeds (and then only after a slow and laborious evolution) in integrating the past into the pure "now" that is his own domain —the only dimension of time that he truly possesses, the only one he has known how to make his. The essential tragedy of all his characters, from Harry Morgan to the bullfighters of

Men Without Women, is that of being confined, imprisoned, in this "now"—all the words for which Robert Jordan finds so poor and inadequate[4] in relation to its living fullness, but the reality of which seems so derisory to the hero of "The Snows of Kilimanjaro" once he feels his life reduced to it.

Most of the specific aspects of Hemingway's art—its limitations as well as its excellences—can be explained by using this central drama of time as a point of departure. Hemingway's successes are of two kinds: those that damn us and those that save us. To the first category belong all the moments when he succeeds in communicating to us with an overwhelming intensity this impression of a blocked destiny: the story of Finito, Pilar's tubercular lover; or the opening short story of the collection *Men Without Women*, "The Undefeated," in which we *know* from the beginning that the old and sick matador will be mortally and ingloriously wounded, that he cannot win. These are his negative successes.

The positive moments are those sections of his work in which, by a kind of heroic effort that is not always crowned with success, he is able to concentrate all the force of the past in a single minute, in the pure "now" that he has always looked for and which is for one moment—though it is on the verge of falling vertiginously into the nothingness of a future impossible to imagine, of collapsing like the wave that has arrived at its supreme point of turgescence—exalted to the

---

[4] "I suppose it is possible to live as full a life in seventy hours as in seventy years, granted that your life has been full up to the time the seventy hours start and that you have reached a certain age. . . . So if your life trades its seventy years for seventy hours I have that value now and I am lucky enough to know it. And if there is not any such thing as a long time, nor the rest of your lives, nor from now on, but there is only now, why then now is the thing to praise and I am very happy with it. Now, *ahora, maintenant, heute.* Now, it has a funny sound to be a whole world and your life. *Esta noche*, tonight, *ce soir, heute abend.*" [Ernest Hemingway, *For Whom the Bell Tolls*, p. 166.]

dimension of eternity. This is true of the two previously mentioned stories, "The Snows of Kilimanjaro" and "Francis Macomber," about which could also be said what Maurice Blanchot so accurately and felicitously said about *For Whom the Bell Tolls*: that at every moment of the narrative "the tranquil present of history is introduced into the breathless present of tragedy," and that, in addition, "the more complicated and precipitate the action becomes, the more the tragedy profits from this contraction of the time span, a contraction that raises feelings and actions to such a tension that we are nailed to our place, immobilized before the present instant . . . and at the same time implacably projected toward a denouement so inevitable that it has already been lived by everyone.[5]

Robert Jordan's inner time is not, as was that of the hero of *A Farewell to Arms*, a jerky and inharmonious time, broken up into a series of discontinuous impulses, but a weighty time, a heavy time (the very rhythm of the narrative surprises us by its slowness and gravity—quite obvious in comparison with the briskness of the narration in *A Farewell to Arms*). Jordan has succeeded in holding in suspension within himself the duration of an existence. His whole life (even his ancestral past, the destiny of his grandfather) is at every moment reintegrated into and brought to bear on whatever he is in the act of accomplishing—on his constantly renewed decision to remain with the Republicans and accomplish his mission (quite probably like what Kierkegaard calls repetition).[6] But this time has no future: the catastrophe that will

[5] *L'Arche* (17), "Traduit de . . ."

[6] Just as the *amor fati* that makes Jordan act as he does is nothing but the consciousness of the profound bond between himself and his condition—what Jaspers defines so well by saying: "Insofar as I act I am not to myself an other in terms of the situations in which I would only be on the outside; what I would be without them is only an empty representation; I am myself in them" (*Philosophie*, II, p. 217).

unfailingly engulf the instant is always imminent; it will happen at the end of the narrative, but we know from the beginning that it is not possible to escape it. Of the three classical dimensions, those that Heidegger calls "the three ecstacies of time," only two, the past and the present, are reconciled. The moment is not eternity, and all the marvels of Hemingway's art cannot make of it a satisfactory equivalent.

This is undoubtedly the central misfortune of which the novelistic work of Hemingway is the "cipher," in the sense of Jaspers and, before him, of Valéry: the veiled incarnation of an inexpressible truth; an ensemble of concrete structures through which (as through the great philosophic systems or the paintings of Van Gogh) is revealed the unexplained and inexplicable significance of Being.

Even leaving aside the work's strictly literary merits, its success is explained easily enough by its "exemplary" value if we remember that the modern mind experiences with a special intensity this drama of time (basic to human consciousness) constantly in danger of being reduced to one of these "ecstacies." Jean Wahl notes, with his customary profundity, that the question of "the moment"—which has haunted the spirits of philosophers and writers since Plato—is especially preoccupying to modern man, most likely because it is a substitute for the eternity there has been no hope of since the "death of God."[7] In an absolutely atheistic universe such as Hemingway's, the drama of time is necessarily lived with intensity, because in such a universe it is not possible for man to have true salvation (since that would signify access to an

---

[7] ". . . from the moment of the third hypothesis (of Parmenides) to the instantaneous pleasure of Aristippus, reconsidered by Walter Pater and André Gide, to the theological moment (moment of incarnation, moment of resurrection, moment of the last judgment *in ictu oculi*), to the moment of Kierkegaard, of Dostoyevsky, to the Nietzschean eternal return that sanctifies the moment, to the eternity of Rimbaud . . ." (Jean Wahl, *Existence humaine et transcendance*, p. 24).

eternity one has even stopped believing in) but only seda-
tives, palliatives, repatchings of the notion of duration—which
is, in all idolatries, fraudulently substituted for the hope of
eternity.

Hemingway's myth of the aggressively virile man,
crushed on all sides by society or destiny and making a firm
stand against them by savagely taking refuge in the pleasures
of the moment, seems then to be a temporary compensatory
solution for an unhappiness that is all too real, all too irreme-
diable, all too universal. The compensatory nature of this
solution is responsible for the principal shortcoming of his
work, one that often spoils it (especially in the period of falling
off and hardening that ends with *To Have and Have Not*):
this is a sentimentality (not, of course, in the conventional
sense of the word) that is more than anything else self-
indulgent—a too-tender regard, full of anticipatory pity, for
his own emotions, his own unhappiness. Under the mask of
the hero that Hemingway submits for our admiration, we catch
an occasional glimpse of a poor little boy (a bit of a spoiled
child) who camouflages himself as a "tough guy" while pam-
pering himself and who soothes himself with heroic reveries
to escape his awareness of a perfectly real misfortune. But
he knows how to soothe us too, and that is why, despite whatever reservations one may have about the lasting efficacy—or
legitimacy—of the relief he brings us, we are carried away by
the magic and caught up by the prestigious mirage he creates
in front of our eyes each time he is in full command of his
technique, of those privileged moments when time sparkles
and the dream makes itself known.

8 *Steinbeck, or the Limits of the Impersonal Novel*

Steinbeck already seems much less important in the history of American literature than he did several years ago, and a novel such as *The Wayward Bus* will certainly not restore his prestige. Yet his very faults have an exemplary significance: his works are representative of the modern American novel at its best—and at its most limited.

Steinbeck's most immediate attraction lies in the extreme simplicity of his art, attested to even by the choice of his novelistic contrivances: the social milieu of his characters, their intellectual level, their very limited vocabulary. A scarcely more extensive vocabulary is used by the author in his narrative passages.

The collection of stories entitled *The Long Valley* more or less epitomizes Steinbeck's work. The stories are not the slightest bit disparate: their relationship is attested to by the title, which unifies them but which is not used for any one of them. United to begin with by a common tone and atmosphere, they are even more bound by at least one of the three

unities classically considered indispensable to tragedy—that
of place. Varying considerably in length, subject, and narrative technique, the thirteen stories do, however, all take place
in the same area, the one closest to Steinbeck's heart: California's Salinas Valley, where he was born. And the hidden relationship created by this common setting is considerably more
profound than that of mere topographical localization: it is as
if this valley—*his* valley—has particularly inspired him,
obliged him to give the best of himself (or at least the most
basic and representative part of himself) and thus use to the
fullest extent those gifts that make him unique among American novelists.

Historically, Steinbeck is a realistic novelist of the Depression era. He did not, however, live through the economic
crisis (which so profoundly modified Hemingway's inspiration,
for instance) in the implacable, inorganic world of the big
cities, but among the gentle landscapes of the "long valley," in
the mild California climate and amid the peace of its vast
orchards. This is what is responsible for the note of serenity
that is never absent from his stories, regardless of the objective
bleakness of the events he recounts. It is impossible for him to
achieve a realism as sordid, a despair as absolute, as that
which marks, for example, James T. Farrell's novels about the
corrupt, urban childhood of young Lonigan.

Simplicity, ease, tenderness—these are the words that
come to mind in characterizing his art. What we like about
his work is that it is so spontaneously in accord with the profound rhythms of natural life (without the pantheism of a
Giono—that Italian writer who cannot sleep for thinking of
the D'Annunzian laurels—which always has something
strained and emphatic about it) yet capable of elevating the
moderation of its tone to the epic (and undoubtedly somewhat simplistic) protest against capitalist society of *The
Grapes of Wrath*.

Evil in Steinbeck is always unambiguous: man is by nature good, and one might say that the sight of the California orchards has given him the same kind of optimism without servility that Rousseau got from the vineyards of Clarens. In the very rhythm of his style one feels the peaceful assurance of a man who walks through the countryside, *his* countryside, at a regular pace, sure of arriving at a night's resting place no matter where it may be; thanks to this assurance, he can skirt the abysses of existence without panic. He can come up against the scandals of American society (as in *In Dubious Battle*) without ending up with the weariness of a Dos Passos; he can, in the course of the stories that make up *The Long Valley*, contemplate with an unwavering eye the depths of the human soul—give us the story of a *crime passionel* in "The Murder," show us a man returning from a lynching in "The Vigilante," or a sadist who feeds a snake live rats in "The Snake"—without upsetting us unduly or making us despair of mankind.

There is in Steinbeck a kind of Eden-like saintliness, a pre-Adam innocence, which is due to the fact that the domain in which he most easily moves is that of the infrahuman. Contact with his books (not imitations of them) cannot help but be enriching and refreshing for a literature as passionately, almost as exclusively, concerned with the individual and his psychological complexities as is French literature. Creator of the unforgettable Lennie, the retarded giant of *Of Mice and Men* who strangles mice and women though he only wants to caress them, Steinbeck seems incapable of portraying human beings in their individuality as men; he sees them only in their animality or as members of a mass in which they meld together and cease to be themselves. The moments of extreme emotion in *The Long Valley* are found, for example, in "Breakfast," in which some starving men eat bacon and drink coffee; or in "The Chrysanthemums," when Elisa explains to the tramp what she feels in cutting back her flowers as she crushes the condemned buds between her fingers and describes the symbiosis that is then in effect between man and plant. The heroine of "The White Quail" identifies herself with the bird she sees in her garden, finding her deep, real self in this loss of individuality. Indeed, one might use as an epigraph for all Steinbeck's work what the old pioneer, at the conclusion of his Indian stories, says to his grandson Jody in "The Leader of the People":

> I tell these old stories, but they're not what I want to tell. I only know how I want people to feel when I tell them. It wasn't Indians that were important, nor adventures, nor even getting out here. It was a whole bunch of people made into one big crawling beast.[1]

That "whole bunch of people made into one big crawling beast" is what Steinbeck so marvelously knows how to make us feel, whereas French Unanimism, from Charles Vildrac to Jules Romains, has rarely succeeded in this. It is what makes *In Dubious Battle* and *The Grapes of Wrath* so good.

With the latter, Steinbeck managed to achieve—like Dos Passos in *U.S.A.*, but by completely different means—the impersonal novel. Perhaps this separation between generations, this perceptible change of atmosphere as one goes from the compressed style of Faulkner to the rolling periods of Steinbeck, can be explained sociologically rather than biographically. Faulkner and Dos Passos resist the world that surrounds them, bear witness against it as much as they can. It is as if they were employed despite themselves to picture a reality they dislike. This reality, this world-as-it-is, Steinbeck has from the beginning taken hold of, in its grandeur as in its horror. His is a "consonant" personality, as the characterolo-

---

[1] John Steinbeck, *The Long Valley*, New York, Viking, 1938, p. 302.—Tr.

gists say (or, if one prefers, a "syntonic" one, though of a syntony a bit rudimentary in relation to our "schizoid civilization"). He is perfectly attuned to the impersonalism of what he wants to portray, and he does not want to express anything else, while in Dos Passos's prose it always seems as if one can hear the deep mutterings of the impenitent individualist, the old Adam who finds it difficult to resign himself to death. In Dos Passos, it is not only the reader's attention (to say nothing of his affection) that turns so often from the collective reality to a particular character, but also the author's. For Dos Passos, the extreme collectivization of man remains a malediction to the end; Steinbeck knew from the beginning how to make of it his grandeur.

And yet it took ten years for him to arrive at a full awareness of his deep desire to depersonalize the novel, though it is a desire implicit even in his first books. Instead of being centered on individual human beings, these have for their subjects the portrayal of a group: the pirate milieu in *Cup of Gold* (Steinbeck's completely unsuccessful first book, 1929) and the poor in *Tortilla Flat* (1935), which is the name of a populous section of Monterey. *Of Mice and Men* (1937) brings us one step closer to the negation of human individuality by giving us a dual hero formed of the indissoluble union of George and Lennie—man and monster, conscience and animality.[2]

In Dubious Battle was also to be centered on two men —Mac and Jim—bound this time less by personal friendship than by common participation in the same task: the organization of the lumpenproletariat of the United States, that amor-

----

[2] We get a glimpse of this duplication of hero in *Tortilla Flat*, where we have not one but two central characters, Pilon and Danny; this is a union no less indissoluble, but for completely different reasons, than that of Lennie and George—to such a point that the book ends with their separation by Danny's death and deification, whereby he becomes a sort of mythic hero of Tortilla Flat.

phous mass of agricultural workers, of the unemployed, of vagabonds of a hundred different occupations—the floating population that no professional organization ever defends. And the true subject, the true "hero" of the book is not the individual fates of Mac or Jim, but the story of their common task, the fruitpickers' strike; the novel is their *Iliad*, and behind it, beyond it, we can see the outline of an even greater and more impersonal adventure of which this is only one episode. Here Mac and Jim (unlike Dos Passos's Glenn Spotswood, whose impenitent individualism often retains our exclusive attention to the detriment of the proletarian adventure considered as a whole) are nothing but commentators and privileged observers—the consciousnesses that are half doers, half endurers, the participants with whom author and readers must identify in order to contemplate the adventure because the novelist needs a particular consciousness in which to install his camera.

To renounce too abruptly the hero, the traditional "sympathetic character" whose point of view the reader espouses (monogamously), would be to shatter our habits (and the writer's) too brusquely, upset our way of seeing too completely. What defines Mac and Jim, what constitutes their essence, is that they have freed themselves from themselves. They have not been dispossessed of these selves in the purely passive and negative manner of Dos Passos's characters; rather, they have voluntarily renounced their individuality. This is the meaning of the funeral oration Mac pronounces over Jim's body in a last effort to make his friend useful to the Cause—words with which the book ends and which are, in effect, the book's moral: "Comrades, he didn't want nothing for himself . . ."

In *The Grapes of Wrath* the evolution toward impersonalism is even more marked: the book does not have a

"sympathetic character" (or at least one who is *eminently*
that, in the academic sense of the term), a "hero," or even
someone who moves the action forward (as Mac and Jim still
did). The only ones who are a bit more individualized or
particularized than any of the rest are obscure supernumer-
aries, chosen arbitrarily by the novelist, who could be replaced
by others with quite different particularities without any
great damage to the book as a whole. They are simple pawns
on a chessboard, involved in a tragedy that vastly over-
shadows them, that they have not created, that they cannot
surmount.

The basic subject of the book is the odyssey (corresponding to the *Iliad* that was *In Dubious Battle*) of the Oklahoma
migrants, small farmers whose property has been taken over
by the banks because in a capitalist society cotton-growing
must be highly industrialized to be profitable. These people,
dispossessed of their ancestral land and attracted by the false
promises of the large landowners of California, are heading
west to hire themselves out as farmworkers. Steinbeck's artistic
effort is to put before us the drama of this completely impersonal being constituted by their social group—this "being
on the march," as it were, in the strictest sense of the term.

Since a writer must work within novelistic traditions, he
most often shows us his tragedy by means of the story of
one of the units that make up the collectivity, the kind of
novelistic atom (already transindividual) that is constituted
by the Joad family. But this sometimes seems a simple con-
cession made to our habits as readers: there are entire chapters (and not the least successful ones) in which the focus
is not at all on the Joads but on anonymous individuals—who
are in any case exactly (or almost exactly) like them. Only
when one of them is addressed by name, or when a direct
allusion to a specific fact of his life is made, do we understand that we are not still concerned with one of the habitual

protagonists of the drama—and that it is not very important.[3]

Thus, one of the most aesthetically harmonious chapters of the book has only the most tenuous (not to say imperceptible) relationship to the plot as such: it describes several hours' experience in one of the gas stations dotting the country's interminable, straight-as-an-arrow highways. There in succession come the truck drivers to drink and talk, the rich people in their beautiful cars to refresh themselves disdainfully (more in an effort to amuse themselves than out of real need), and also, from time to time, one of the migrants who cannot make it (lack of money or gas) to the next town and timidly tries to buy a piece of bread. (We are free to think, if we wish, that it is Tom Joad.) The narrative is interspersed with didactic chapters in which the collective being is presented to us directly, in which it is the collective entity of dispossessed farmers that is the actual subject of the book. Nothing "happens," if you will, during these pages (for that matter, little enough "happens" during the entire course of the book, given its length), yet they are not for that the less necessary for the whole—but poetically rather than novelistically.

Because the epic interest takes precedence over the novelistic interest, the book does not "finish"—that is, it ends without Steinbeck having told us what has happened to the main characters or even what will happen to the mass of migrants. Even in *In Dubious Battle* the last lines of the book leave us uncertain about Mac's future after Jim's death, and about the final result of the strike that has been the subject

---

[3] The method, in terms of its effect, is exactly comparable to Dos Passos's use of the Camera Eye. The interest is displaced, without our specifically being made aware of it (just as in an Orson Welles film when the spectator's attention is focused on the middle ground or background) from one of the central characters to an anonymous extra. We are brusquely introduced into the consciousness of Mr. Whoever—Heidegger's *"Mann"* if you wish—and it is his life, his interior monologue, that we are given.

of the book. Individuals pass on; the group (or the Cause) remains. The strike itself (as Mac says many times in the course of the book) is only a moment in the organization of the proletariat, a single panel of an immense fresco that Steinbeck, limited by the very restrictions of his art, can show us only a part of; lost or won, the strike is almost an anecdotal detail. As for what happens to Mac, he is even less important; whether he falls by the wayside or goes elsewhere to organize the masses of unskilled workers, this also will not appreciably affect the final outcome.

In the same way, *The Grapes of Wrath* ends with an image that is purely poetic and does not in the least put a final period to the plot: Steinbeck shows us "Rose of Sharon" (the Joads' biblically named youngest daughter), who has just had a stillborn child, breastfeeding a man found by her mother during a torrential rainfall—a man dying of hunger, whose ruined stomach can digest nothing but milk, which no one has the money to buy for him. Steinbeck's Eden-like simplicity, about which I spoke earlier, can be better appreciated if one compares the archaic ingenuousness with which he handles a situation that could so easily be scabrous with the lewdness (hidden under a false objectivity) of an analogous story by Maupassant.

We are not told what has happened to Tom, the oldest son and protagonist, whom the police are looking for, what the Joad family will do, or even what will happen to the mass of dispossessed farmers. Perhaps this is because a collective entity does not have a story, a personal destiny, in the sense that individuals have one; without an arbiter—inevitable if one wishes to present the story literarily—it is not possible to stop the story of the transformation of this being in march at any given moment. In addition, if the novel no longer has individuals as its subject, it ceases to be an art of narration and becomes an art of description. Like the great Russian movies, and for the same reasons, novels tend more and more to be documentaries that merely *show* the impersonal reality of which they speak, without *recounting it.*

One gets a glimpse here, in its earliest stages, of a growing tendency on the part of the great American writers to lose their interest in fiction and turn toward a kind of reportage mingled with abstract considerations: Dos Passos in *The Ground We Stand On* and *State of the Nation;* Erskine Caldwell in *Some American People* and (in conjunction with the photographs of Margaret Bourke-White) *You Have Seen Their Faces.* At the same time we can also see the danger inherent in works of this kind: they lack novelistic interest for the reader, just because they are not tied to a plot. Steinbeck's temptation is the "arabesque," the detail lovingly lingered over for its own sake, just as the "beautiful image" is the danger for the skillful director or the one too much in love with his craft.

From this point of view it is instructive to compare the story "Breakfast" with another version of the same episode that is incorporated in *The Grapes of Wrath.* It concerns a very simple episode: the narrator, at dawn, discovers a campfire where two men are preparing their breakfast while a young woman is nursing her child, and they invite him to share their meal. But over and beyond the simple and intense pleasure of eating and the sudden communion established among them, it seems to the hero that the scene is pregnant with a profound poetry that he cannot elucidate, that he cannot communicate to the reader; and the writer, conscious of having failed in his mission—which is exactly that of expressing the inexpressible, of bringing to light and communicating the ineffable—ends his story with an awkward and embarrassed confession: "That's all. I know, of course, some of the reasons why it was pleasant. But there was some element of great beauty there that makes the rush of warmth when I think of it."

On the other hand, when in *The Grapes of Wrath* the same scene is connected with the main character, Tom, when it is incorporated into his life and not just presented as an image of beauty, sufficient unto itself, Steinbeck no longer has any need to underline its poetic significance in intellectual terms. Because of its context, the episode as a whole has an inner meaning, and its inherent beauty comes through on its own. Nothing—no scene, no story—is moving in itself; it becomes so only in relation to the eyes and the consciousness that perceive it. (Individualistic and "petit bourgeois" art at least had the merit of remaining human—alas, sometimes too human.) Steinbeck can speak better of animals and plants, or orchards and mice, than of men, so his art is perpetually threatened by the gravest danger facing the impersonal novel —dehumanization.

This same impersonalism is, however, also responsible for the essential merits of this art: its grandeur and its serenity. It is because individual existence is not important that the denouements of both *Of Mice and Men* and *In Dubious Battle* are not, for all their violence, sad: they are part of the order of things. It does not really matter if Jim is killed or if the strike fails (as a matter of fact, Mac knows from the beginning that it is destined to fail); things go on, a bit better because of Jim's sacrifice—which is not even a sacrifice since it is not a true loss. Jim does not value himself; his life takes on meaning only when he joins the party, for it is only then that he begins to exist.

Malraux's characters, on the other hand (and it is with Malraux that Steinbeck can best be compared), have a personal existence that is almost too strong. They know that life is unique and that it is all man possesses. When they sacrifice it, there is true anguish, true tragedy, even if the tragedy and the anguish both remain mute. They are still involved with the human; it is their personal story that forms the web of the narrative. If they manage to rid themselves of their individuality, as Kotov does at the end of *La Condition humaine*, we see this evolution unfolding before our eyes; we are not spared one step of the calvary. In Steinbeck, however, the characters' depersonalization has taken place before the story begins, either because their inner ascesis is complete, as is true of Mac and Jim, or because, like the Joads, they have never attained consciousness of their separate individuality— because, in other words, they are infraindividuals.

Malraux's greatness is thus diametrically opposed to Steinbeck's, and the difference is reflected even in the rhythm of their styles: a rhythm of harmony in Steinbeck, a rhythm of insistence and despair in Malraux. The overwhelming grandeur of the end of *La Condition humaine*, or of Hernandez's death in *L'Espoir* (*Man's Hope*), comes from the author's belief that physical suffering and death are real and *irreparable*. Because Steinbeck has the profound indifference of nature toward human suffering, he can allow himself to write scenes that would be all but intolerable in another author. For example, in *In Dubious Battle* we find Mac sympathetic despite the scene in which he systematically and without anger, simply because he has to, beats and disfigures an adolescent—hardly more than a child—who cannot defend himself.

The basic subject of *Of Mice and Men*, expressed abstractly, is atrocious, but tragedy has disappeared even from the final scene; what emerges is only a kind of abstract pity for the human condition, a little like that sometimes communicated to us by Shakespeare. In Malraux or Dos Passos, however, we do not for one moment stop seeing the characters' suffering as metaphysically *inexpiable*. In the "Epistle to John Hamilton Reynold" Keats speaks of a sort of "Purgatory blind . . . "—made up of helpless pity for the pain of the universe—which all artists must cross. It seems as if Steinbeck and his characters have emerged from it, while Malraux and Dos Passos are still within it.

Because there is no element of metaphysical rebellion in Steinbeck, his social preoccupations show a very different emphasis: we are not tempted to feel pity for Mac or Jim, for they are from the beginning beyond the reach of anything that may happen to them. They have a kind of royal calm that is almost without parallel except in some of Shakespeare's characters—for example, Mark Antony in *Antony and Cleopatra*. Steinbeck has succeeded in completely effecting the transfiguration of all the horrible, ugly, or vulgar elements of reality to the point where they do not even seem ugly or horrible except to the abstract intellect that arbitrarily isolates them from their literary expression. This also explains the admirable use Steinbeck makes of slang, clichés, what seems to be the most debased and vulgar kind of language—all of which allow him to express better than any austere intellectual vocabulary the large simple truths: virile fraternity, death, communism, heroism, charity. In Steinbeck, nothing of daily existence can shock us, for from the beginning we are beyond such considerations. Like Keats, Steinbeck, in refusing evasion, has found the best refuge—absolute immanence.

At this point we should analyze the literary techniques that make this transfiguration possible. One of these would be the internal rhythm of the work—for example, the fugal technique of *Of Mice and Men*, with its regular responses of subject and countersubject. Balzac was proud of having composed one of his novels as Rossini might have; one might say that *Of Mice and Men* is composed like Bach, and that in it Steinbeck attains the same serene gravity.

But this is only true of his successes, of the privileged moments of his work. In every author there is a central point from which flow both the defects and the virtues of his work. In Steinbeck this center of gravity is infrahuman impersonalism. The fundamental ambiguity of his work derives from the fact that one never knows if his characters are beyond clear self-awareness and distinct individuality or if they have never reached it; and though this ambiguity is quite real in the case of Mac and Jim, it is obviously not at all so for Lennie (*Of Mice and Men*), or for the idiot of the story called "Johnny Bear," or for Pilon and Danny (*Tortilla Flat*), or for the toughs of *Cannery Row*, who are simply and unequivocally a bit below average humanity, not at all transcendent in relation to it.

Herein lies the essential limitation of Steinbeck's art. His extraordinary ability to capture and portray as a function of man his most elementary (and hence, it would seem, most essential) determinants—those that separate him least from his fellow men and even from other creatures—ends by working against him. Both the collapse of his syntax, incapable of expressing even the least abstract logical relationship, and the poverty of his vocabulary (not a deliberate poverty, as in Racine, but one that derives from the nature of the subject or the ability of the artist—and which of these it is, is irrelevant), singularly restrict his area of expression. Faced with the extraordinarily rudimentary language used by his main characters (and often, as if by contagion, by the narrator), one is reminded of the statement of the American critic Margaret Thorp:

> A student of the American language once made an exhaustive study of the vocabulary of these constant writers to the fan magazines. Each letter writer, he found, has at her command, for the expression of the whole gamut of rapture and disgust, just one hundred and fifty words.[4]

[4] Margaret Farrand Thorp, *America at the Movies*, New Haven, Yale University Press, 1939, p. 98.

Or else one thinks of the apes studied by Kohler (apes who had at most fifteen onomatopoeic sounds with which to express their range of emotions), or, finally, of the comments of d'Etiemble:

> With 850 words of English and some rules of grammar, there has been constructed a lingua franca whose poverty the Anglo Saxons hope will enable it to conquer the globe. This is Basic English. The Bible and Shakespeare have been rewritten, using only the 850 words thus selected—if one can use that expression. As *The New York Times* (or is it *The London Times?*) said: "From now on Shakespeare will be grand reading for everybody."

Whoever rewrites Steinbeck's books will certainly have less trouble than the "translator" of the Bible or *Madame Bovary*.

If Steinbeck's characters only rarely achieve full novelistic reality, it is precisely because they are so little individualized, so little individual, and, finally, so little human. Their emotions, situated as they are below the diaphragm or centered around the solar plexus, remain forever obscure and opaque; it is hard to imagine these characters ever arriving at—in no matter how distant a future—a clear understanding of themselves. Naturally, their creator fails as soon as he tries to portray more complex individuals such as one does, after all, meet in modern civilization. This is most likely why *The Moon Is Down* is an abstract book, too simplistic to be convincing, and semicaricatural (involuntarily)—a book in which almost nothing rings true, especially to European ears.

Morever, there is a terrible lack in Steinbeck's universe —what Denis de Rougemont so aptly called the "devil's share," or, to use a less explicitly theological language, the sense of evil. To think about his work is to find additional meaning in the terrible and prophetic words of Walter Rathenau: " 'America has no soul,' has not deserved to have one, for she has not yet 'deigned to plunge into the abyss of suffering and sin.' "[5]

(At this point one should observe that there is a mystery, probably historic in essence, that goes beyond literature and touches on the very nature of contemporary American civilization: the mystery of the disappearance of this "sense of evil"—so deep and so sharp in Hawthorne and Melville—from the modern American consciousness. The collective soul seems to have strongly repressed it after the middle of the nineteenth century—a repression that largely explains the total failure with its contemporary public of that part of Melville's work which today seems to us the most important, from *Moby Dick* to *Billy Budd*, and a repression that is also the most likely explanation for the fact that the United States proved impossible to live in for Henry James and T. S. Eliot, who could not find there the spiritual climate necessary to them.)

Without undertaking the psychoanalysis of the American soul necessary to elucidate this mystery, and returning to the level of literary criticism in general and Steinbeck in particular, I can at least say that his characters' very innocence is ultimately somewhat suspect and false—certainly somewhat monstrous. Lennie's sadism, or *Schadenfreude* (whatever name we wish to give it), may be made literarily acceptable because he is unaware of it; that does not make it the less atrocious—nor Lennie's death either, for that matter. Similarly, the falsely picaresque aspect of the adventures recounted in *Tortilla Flat* or *Cannery Row* are not amusing for very long. Twentieth-century man cannot with impunity, without fundamental damage to his being, reduce himself to life on the physical level alone.

In addition, because of this same amputation, Steinbeck's

[5] Cited by André Gide in his *Journal*, trans. by Justin O'Brien, New York, Alfred A. Knopf, 1951, Vol. 2, p. 283.—Tr.

universe and the artistic domain in which he achieves his successes are both necessarily limited. His usual means of expression desert him as soon as he tries to evoke anything other than the farmworkers of California, the pioneers of the eighteenth-century West, or the tramps of Monterey: a universe of sadists, vagabonds, and congenital cretins. We are almost happy when he openly and frankly returns to the portrayal of pure animal nature. It is no accident that the best stories of *The Long Valley* have as their true "heroes," their centers of attention and sympathy, animals rather than men, and are called "The White Quail," "The Snake," and "The Red Pony." But one may well ask if there are great possibilities open to an "animal novelist," no matter how perfect his art, no matter how deep the sympathy that unites him to his subjects.

9 *Faulkner, or Theological Inversion*

"I am not sure," says Alain in his *Propos de littérature,* "that beautiful works please. It seems to me that it would sometimes be more accurate to say that they displease. They grab at one, and without permission. Admiration is not a pleasure, perhaps, but rather a kind of attention. . . . " And Alain applies these remarks to Balzac's works, in which "the reader is neither spared, nor flattered, nor reassured; no one cares if he is pleased or not . . . " to such a point that one would occasionally like to "punish this impolite art by mockery or rejection."

There is among contemporary American novelists an author as basically shocking, as unconcerned about the reader's pleasure or opinion, as Balzac, a writer whose other traits—even more noteworthy than their common impoliteness—also allow us to compare him with Balzac. This novelist is William Faulkner. Like Balzac, and even more than Balzac, he is deliberately obscure, sometimes deliberately boring, and never more inimitable, more inexorably faithful to himself than when he makes the fewest concessions and dares be obscure or boring to the maximum degree.

It is impossible to ascribe to awkward technique, to the inexperience of the novice, those particularities that are accentuated in the works of his maturity. *Mosquitoes* and *Soldiers' Pay* have a simple construction and are easily accessible in comparison with *Absalom, Absalom!* or *The Wild Palms,*[1] the first of which is disconcerting, the second almost repugnant. Just as the hidden economy of *La Comédie humaine* can be seen in such essential elements as the first forty pages of the description of Guérande at the beginning of *Béatrix* or the most melodramatic aspects of *l'Histoire des treize* (*The Thirteen*), so the apparent narrative perversity of Faulkner's tales can be seen as justified, not to say inevitable, if one understands its hidden significance.

There are three obvious singularities in Faulknerian art. The first of these is his inability to tell a story other than by beginning at the end and then going back in time (three examples: the story "Wash"; the beginning of *The Wild Palms*, where we are first shown the dying woman in a garden; and especially *Absalom, Absalom!*, where we are gradually immersed in a hundred-year-old past spanning three generations). The second singularity is his need always to tell at least two stories simultaneously (often jumping without warning from one to another, as when, in *Light in August*, the story goes thirty years back in time to concern itself with a baby who will turn out to be the hero, Joe Christmas), either juxtaposed, as the stories of the convict and of the doctor are in *The Wild Palms*, or, more often, interwoven in ways that may vary but are nevertheless always subtle and sometimes very hidden, as in the story "Mistral," (in *These*

---

[1] The first two are from 1927 and 1926 respectively, the two others from 1936 and 1939. In the interval Faulkner published seven books, and not unimportant ones: *Sanctuary* and *Light in August* are among them.

Thirteen) or in *Pylon*, where the story of the contemporary event (the aviation meet) is intertwined with the story of past events that are slowly made clear (the relationships of Laverne and the two men who live with her). Finally, there is his taste for conundrums, which is carried to perversion, almost to childishness, and which makes him give the same name of Quentin to the uncle and the niece, and that of Caddy to the mother and the daughter,[2] and even to hide from us to the end the name of the reporter in *Pylon*, a name about which we know only that it is so ridiculous as to bring forth bursts of mad laughter from everyone who hears it. Other examples of these different narrative techniques can be found in almost any one of Faulkner's books; I have chosen these few extremely striking examples at random. If to all this is added the deliberate resolve never to mention a crucial event (the murder of Sutpen in "Wash," or that of Wash Jones's granddaughter), and, if possible, to hide from us even the knowledge of it (the famous rape in *Sanctuary*, or Joe Christmas's black blood), the end result is an assemblage of oddities that reinforce each other until the ordinary reader is made to oscillate from migraine to irritation. In the end, the least prejudiced, most well-disposed mind is led to accusations of deliberate, overelaborate affectation.

I have not yet discussed the purely stylistic singularities that add to and reinforce the narrative anomalies: the immoderate use of qualifying adjectives (usually four or five of them) which makes the translator's task so difficult, if not impossible;[3] and, even more important, the length of the sentences and the incidents that go on interminably (com-

[2] In *The Sound and the Fury*. [Magny is wrong: the mother's name is Caroline; the daughter is Candace.—Tr.]

[3] I take at random the second line of *Absalom, Absalom!* "the long still hot weary dead September afternoon . . .": four adjectives, one of which is modified by an adverb, for the same noun.

pared to Faulkner, Proust and Charles du Bos are very short-winded authors). Burdened with more richness than man's spirit can bear, the best-intentioned reader must flounder. I will cite only two examples. The first is in the long short story "The Bear," included in *Go Down, Moses*; the fourth and most difficult part includes a two-page parenthesis embedded in a six-page sentence. The second example is in *The Portable Faulkner*. At the request of Malcolm Cowley, the editor, Faulkner added to this anthology an appendix, which is very revealing and about which I will have more to say. It is a collection of biographies about the Compsons, and the biography of Quentin (the last one, the daughter of Caddy-Candace) includes a two-page parenthetical explanation of the events that make up the last part of *The Sound and the Fury*, this time differently explained and developed, but no more intelligible than in the original version. These two texts are even more interesting in that both of them give us the impression of catching the narrative genius of Faulkner in the act, *in flagrante delictu*; he cannot help but immediately obscure whatever he touches, for his narrative method is in essence *enveloping* and implicative rather than developmental and discursive.

This does not keep the reader from being tempted to cry mercy—or from protesting against the uncustomary effort expected of him by accusing the author of being arbitrary and even perverse. We all know the famous (most likely legendary) anecdote about Mallarmé adding obscurity to verses that seemed to lack it. It sometimes seems as though Faulkner has used his methods mischievously—not to disentangle his story and make it clearer (in any case, more readable), but to further mislead the innocent and unfortunate reader and "add obscurity" to a reality that must still have seemed to him too ordered, insufficiently chaotic.

Time, the Moloch

Of course, the perversity is only on the surface. The idea is born of our irritation, yet it is partly true. First of all, Faulkner does not in fact much concern himself, when he writes, with his eventual reader. Malcolm Cowley, in his Introduction to *The Portable Faulkner* (a collection he compiled with Faulkner's cooperation), vividly describes the author's attitude toward the public as being a mixture of "skittery distrust and pure unconsciousness that the public exists." He gives many examples of this, among them Faulkner's indifference both about the spelling of his name (with or without a "u") and about the erroneous information occasionally published about his life. Cowley also notes that once a book is finished, Faulkner loses all interest in it—and even in the details of its publication—to such a degree that he sometimes does not even keep a copy of it for himself. The most likely reason for this is what he explained in one of his letters: "I think I have written a lot and sent it off to print before I actually realized strangers might read it." His novels, especially the early ones, are much more stories he might have told himself (as children do) than narratives composed for others. That explains why he is so little concerned with making them intelligible or even simply readable.

Still, all this is only a partial explanation, and even more so in that, as we have already noted, his latest books, written in an intellectual solitude necessarily less complete than before, are even more inaccessible—if that is possible—than his first. Actually, since the narrative complexity of Faulkner's tales is not a deficiency but rather a positive quality, it cannot be explained in purely negative terms—that is, as a result of the author's technical awkwardness or his indifference to the reader; in that case, it would not have the right to expect our tolerance. I hope to show that it is not accidental but deliberate; that it bears a strong, indissoluble relationship to the vision of the world Faulkner wishes to communicate; and that this basic relationship is responsible for its significance and its value.

All those who have studied Faulkner have noted the strange transformation that Time undergoes in his narratives. Sartre in particular has devoted an article to this aspect of *The Sound and the Fury*,[4] and Jean Pouillon returns to this same question several times in his study *Temps et Roman* as well as in his treatment of *Pylon* in *Les Temps Modernes* (No. 13). The most striking characteristic of the Faulknerian novel is that the course of the narrative is continually being blocked (especially by interminable parenthetical remarks and interpolations) and that it furthermore almost always, because of varying kinds of artifices, unwinds in reverse, going from the present to the past (*Absalom, Absalom!* is a typical example) instead of, as would be more normal, from the present to the future. Each episode, by its obscurity, refers back to another, often twenty or thirty years earlier. To understand Sutpen's opposition to his daughter Judith's marriage with his son Henry's best friend, and to understand the strange attraction that both Judith and Henry feel toward that enigmatic and attractive Charles Bon, we must know about certain events that took place in Haiti thirty years before: we must know that Charles Bon, son of Sutpen's first marriage to a creole of mixed blood, is Judith and Henry's half brother and that he has colored blood.

Similarly, we go thirty years back in time in *Light in August*, and the adventures of a little boy in an orphan asylum are the key to all Joe Christmas's subsequent behavior. There

---

[4] The essay, originally appearing in *La Nouvelle Revue Française*, was reissued as a note on *Sartoris* in the volume entitled *Situations I* (Gallimard).

are many such examples. The important thing is that Faulkner systematically takes leave of official chronology (from which derives the symbolic importance, very well interpreted by Sartre, of Quentin's breaking his watch or of the idiot Benjy's inability to tell time). Faulkner himself wants to ignore clock time in order to substitute for it living time, true time—that is, not time as we commonly know it, oriented toward the future and, so to speak, drawn toward it, but time as a fixed past, overhanging the actual minute with the immobility of a cyclopean wall and preextracting all reality from it.

Sartre has shown, in discussing *Sartoris*, that Faulkner does not allow events to appear in his story except after they have happened; as in *The Sound and the Fury*, "everything happens behind the scenes, everything has happened." The same is true of Temple's rape, which is the core of *Sanctuary*. In all these works the present is never anything but a future past, poor and faded in relation to the *true* past, powerless to defend itself against that true past. Even in the consciousness of the characters, who it would seem should be in the process of *living* this present, it ends by being completely masked by earlier events. It will only appear later— almost always in the consciousness of another character—when it has in its turn become a past and acquired a massive immutability. It is like what happens in the case of young Chinese girls, who must wait until they themselves are old, the mothers-in-law and the grandmothers, before they can rule their households. It is as if Faulkner's characters are always one existence behind.

A typical example of this use of time is found in the section of *The Sound and the Fury* that Sartre summarizes as follows: "When Quentin insults Bland, he isn't even aware of it; he is reliving his fight with Dalton Ames. And when Bland hits him, the dispute is covered over and hidden by the past brawl between Quentin and Ames. Later, Shreve will *recount* how Bland hit Quentin: he will *recount* the scene because it has become history. . . . " In other words, the only way for events to be registered in both the protagonists' consciousness and the writer's narrative is for them to have taken place long before; otherwise they do not really *exist*.

Sometimes it happens that we are present when time suddenly solidifies and becomes frozen in the past, when it "takes" like rubber, at the moment the event occurs, but simultaneously isolates itself irremediably from the rest of time:

> . . . he would contemplate the inexplicable and fading fury of the past twenty-four hours circled back to itself and become whole and intact and objective and already vanishing slowly like the damp print of a lifted glass on a bar.[5]

What is more, for one of the characters an event still to happen may seem so ineluctable that it is already in the past: this is what happens to Temple in *Sanctuary* just before Popeye kills Red, her lover:

> He gave her the glass. She drank. When she set the glass down she realized that she was drunk. *She believed that she had been drunk for some time. She thought that perhaps she had passed out and that it had already happened.* She could hear herself saying I hope it has. I hope it has. *Then she believed it had and she was overcome by a sense of bereavement and of physical desire.*[6]

---

[5] William Faulkner, *Pylon*, New York, Harrison Smith and Robert Haas, 1935, p. 201.—Tr.

[6] William Faulkner, *Sanctuary* [New York, New American Library, 1954, pp. 134–35. Italics are Magny's.] In the same way, Tommy's assassination: "To Temple, sitting in the cottonseedhulls and the corncove, the sound was no louder than the striking of a match: a short, minor sound shutting down upon the scene, the instant, with a profound finality, completely isolating it . . ." [Ibid., p. 58].

At most, in Faulkner's universe, some passage (usually very brief) will occasionally give us a momentary glimpse of something that is actually happening: a timeless present briefly and miraculously suspended above the world, a brief gap in the inexorable web of time in which instant ceaselessly overlaps instant. Gowan's automobile accident at the beginning of *Sanctuary* is an example. "The engine ceased, though the lifted front wheel continued to spin idly, slowing." Or, as is said in "All the Dead Pilots" as a kind of funeral oration for John Sartoris: "The courage, the recklessness, call it what you will, is the flash, the instant of sublimation; then flick! the old darkness again." Then one falls back into the concrete universe of inflexible and changeless things, those about which there is no story. "A one-inch sliver of sulphur-tipped wood is longer than memory or grief; a flame no larger than a sixpence is fiercer than courage or despair." Only the past is real, because only the past enables the subjective and changing event to *really* exist, as things exist.

Not only is the present not known, but it can never be known. One never sees it: one does not see what is in the process of happening at the moment in which it is happening; one sees only the past. Nothing exists but *legend*, which can be told, and which is made to be told. At a certain moment in *Absalom, Absalom!* Quentin Compson *sees* such events as Sutpen's return and the funerary monument he raises for his wife—events that are for him imaginary, long since returned to nothingness—better than if he had been there, and certainly better than he will see his own death, better than he would have been able to see something he might actually have witnessed: " . . . he might even have been there. Then he thought *No. If I had been there I could not have seen it this plain.*"[7] [Faulkner's italics]

    [7] William Faulkner, *Absalom, Absalom!*, New York, Random House, 1951, p. 190.

This is certainly a psychologically incontestable statement: for there to be consciousness and knowledge, there must be registration and reflection. Consciousness, insofar as it is by nature and necessity consciousness-of-consciousness, thus seems turned toward the past—but only toward the immediate past, which explains, among other things, the forgetfulness, in traumatic amnesias, of the events immediately preceding the accident and the resultant loss of consciousness. On a more banal level, it also explains the regular and as it were statutory concealment of the moment at which one falls asleep.

But Faulkner's use of the consciousness of the past goes infinitely beyond the simple scope of psychological observation. He is sure that a person's true reality does not reside, as common sense would have it, in the actions he is completing or the feeling he is experiencing *now*, but that it is completely situated in the past, whether it is his own past or that of his race. Faulkner finds the impossibility of ever grasping the present in relation to the conditions that make for consciousness of it enough to bring in a verdict of nonreality as concerns that present. In Kantian language, he makes a transcendent use of what is only the transcendental form of knowledge. He gives us *legend* as sole truth.

Because the characters in his stories regard the past so persistently, they allow themselves to be bewitched and devoured by it; it sometimes seems as if they willingly give it permission to overwhelm them. They consent to this Moloch —or rather, the author, their father, consents for them. They think of themselves as completed existences. "I am not, I was," says one of them. Quentin anticipates his suicide, Caddy her shame, Christmas his lynching; Sutpen "gets himself killed," one might say, by Wash Jones (in the story "Wash"); and Temple refuses to leave the bootlegger's house while there is still enough time to do so. Their common attitude can be symbolized by that of the Negro Nancy (in the story "That Evening Sun") seated by the fire in her lonely cabin, sure that her husband, Jesus, is coming to kill her, and passively waiting for him as if she consents to it in advance. They have no rest until their lives have become destiny. Their eyes fixed on a past that has succeeded in encircling even the future they no longer believe in, they await with a kind of hope in hopelessness[8] the unforeseeable and inevitable catastrophe that will burst upon them—all the while lulling themselves with spellbinding tales of ancestral glories.

It is certainly possible to protest against such alienation of man from his freedom—Sartre has done so—and possible also to indicate the arbitrary and partial nature of this Faulknerian view of man and the world by noting, for example, that if consciousness is reflection and retrospection, it is also at the same time, and just as fundamentally, *projection*, turned toward the future as well as toward the past; to reduce it solely to its first aspect is to load the dice. There is thus something specious, not to say insidious, in the narrative technique chosen by Faulkner, and Sartre is not wrong to speak of it as having a kind of "dishonesty" that aims at making us as blind as the author and infecting us with his particular illness—the loss of a sense of the future, or, in short, the absence of hope. "I fear that the absurdity Faulkner finds in a human life has been put there by him in the first place. It's not that life isn't absurd, but that its absurdity is of a different kind."

The reason Faulkner gives for this despair—the social conditions of present-day life—is inadequate. In any case, it does not explain why we so willingly accept an image of the

---

[8] It is noteworthy that in *Sanctuary* the projects of perhaps the only Faulknerian character who tries to make things happen, the lawyer Horace Benbow, are shown to be derisory or even worse, since if he had not been able to reconstruct the true crime and find Temple, the innocent Goodwin would probably not have been condemned and surely not lynched.

world that is simultaneously so strange and so despairing. *The Wild Palms* and *Light in August* are no more just descriptions of a world dying of old age, in which revolutions are impossible, than *The Castle* and *The Trial* are only mythic transcriptions of the stultifying bureaucracy of the Austro-Hungarian empire. One has to admit—surrendering probability as well as optimism—that the Faulknerian character and his destiny have a certain fascination. And that makes it necessary to pose the problem (too summarily resolved by Sartre) of the profound *meaning* of literature and of the value it can have even when it is most obviously cheating.

The Massacre of the Innocents

Of course, every literary work is more or less a deception, since it attempts to make us accept as the only possible—or at least as the most likely—point of view one that is usually quite disagreeable and in any case unique. In the final analysis, the only reproach Sartre can level against the Faulknerian conception of time is that it is not "true." But its deep significance (and, as a corollary, its interest for the reader) is beyond questions of truth and falsity—beyond even the usual categories of aesthetics. I believe that one could with more reason speak of it as *religious*, though it may seem extraordinary to apply this word to a work so profane in appearance. But perhaps it will seem less surprising if we remember that Faulkner's "legends" take place in the land that produced Negro spirituals and, especially, if we investigate the enigma (so impudent that we quickly lose sight of it) posed by the title *Sanctuary* and by the name, "Temple," of the young girl who is therein violated.

Malraux, in his preface to the French translation of *Sanctuary*, defined Faulkner's art as one of "fascination," and

Sartre speaks, concerning *Sartoris*, of "enchantment," almost of magic. The novel that exercises (in the most elemental way) this irresistible and scandalous attraction on the reader is probably *Absalom, Absalom!*—a story that at first seems quite ordinary and without any particularly intriguing enigmas, and ends with the reader being possessed by the same passion that has enthralled the two narrators, Quentin Compson and his Canadian friend, Shreve.

Shreve thinks he is fascinated by the mystery of the "deep South," which he catches glimpses of through each fissure that reveals the destinies of Miss Rosa, Sutpen, Charles Bon, and the others. Quentin is caught (and those who have previously read *The Sound and the Fury* have no trouble understanding this) by the horror of the incestuous attraction between Judith and Charles Bon (with Henry, the third person, throwing his sister into his friend's—and half-brother's—arms so the latter can accomplish what he, Henry, does not dare contemplate for himself). Quentin is drawn by the magnetism of the crime he has not been able to stop dreaming of in connection with his sister, Caddy. But the true fascination —that felt by us, the readers, who are neither Canadians hypnotized by the South nor adolescents obsessed by the mirage of forbidden loves—is more profound: it is the fascination of the Legend, of majestic, unmoving, fixed Time, gradually revealing itself to mortal eyes as the only image of Eternity they will ever be able to perceive.

Reading Faulkner, one thinks of those long biblical genealogies, simple litanies of Old Testament names repeated to the point of satiety, to the point at which they culminate, on Christmas Eve, in the admirable and antiphonic chorus taken up by all the faithful—the beginning of the Gospel According to Saint Matthew: "Abraham begat Isaac; and Isaac begat Jacob; and Jacob begat Judas and his brethren. . . . And after they were brought to Babylon, Jechonias begat

Salathiel. . . . And Jacob begat Joseph the husband of Mary, of whom was born Jesus, who is called Christ." This genealogy of Christ is like the completion of a series, like a sequence of historic, external moments that have finally culminated in, merged into, an Event that is unique and yet Eternal (since announced from the beginning of time): the birth of the Son of God, the Son of Man—in short, the insertion of History into Eternity.

The seemingly profane novels of Faulkner also seem to prophesy Good News to come; they are something given man to ruminate over, so he can be patient while waiting, for he is condemned to go over and over until the Solstice of Solstices the succession of temporal events that have already been inscribed on the blackboard of History—successions that become, while we wait for the Incarnation when all promises will be kept, the only substitute for the Eternity that the Fall and our ambition to be gods have robbed us of. In the absence of Salvation, Man is temporarily given over to Destiny; he has to be entirely turned toward the past, for there is as yet no future. The Temple of Jerusalem has been profaned, the Sanctuary violated. Nothing of any reality can yet happen, since there has not yet taken place the Event par excellence, the one that marks the beginning of the Return, the moment when the Fall from Grace is reversed, when man can once more turn toward God and begin all over again from zero—if for no other reason but to count those years of history.

The universe Faulkner proposes is thus the world before the Incarnation, completely absorbed in the contemplation of what was, busy marking time, tirelessly scanning the records of past glories. How should it not be a world of despair, since Hope has not yet dawned? And just as the Tenebrae is related to the Resurrection, so is the Nativity to the Massacre of the Innocents—those unjustly massacred, unfortunate beings whom Faulkner represents by Tommy shot to death and Goodwin burned alive (*Sanctuary*); Christmas lynched and Miss Burden strangled (*Light in August*); Nancy devoured by vultures at the bottom of a ditch ("That Evening Sun"); Charlotte, the doctor, and the convict all buried alive in their various destinies (*The Wild Palms*); and Bayard Sartoris vanquished like Icarus ("All the Dead Pilots")—to say nothing of Benjy castrated, Temple violated, and those other victims, less pure in the eyes of the world, like Popeye, Sutpen, or Quentin Compson: all mockingly stricken by punishment disproportionate to their crimes.

It is easy to understand the attraction exercised on Faulkner by the so-recently vanished Indian civilization[9] (the Compson children saw its last vestiges), for it constitutes America's prehistory, so to speak. This world of cruelty and superstitious terrors, in which not only the master's horse and dog are buried with him but his Negro servant as well, appears to him even more *inhuman* than the old biblical civilization, which at least prophesied, even if not soothingly, the coming of Christ, when injustices would perhaps be seen to have a meaning.

The Violation of the Temple

It may seem an exaggeration to look for such theological substructures in Faulkner's work, yet the critics have all been struck by his "puritanism," meaning by that term both his visible disgust before the mystery of sex and his deep-seated misogyny—quite natural in a world in which the Immaculate Virgin has not yet come to reestablish the order of things altered by Eve. Faulkner has at least once expressly referred

[9] See the stories "A Justice" and "Red Leaves" in *These Thirteen*.

to the Bible in one of his titles (*Absalom, Absalom!*)—
precisely the one that most evokes the Hebraic ritual of meditation on the past. In addition, I do not see how—except by
this perpetual referral of contemporary events to a sacred
context that gives them their full meaning—one can explain
the extravagant title of *Sanctuary* given to a story that is sordid to an extreme and whose protagonists are a heredo-
syphilitic, sadistic, and impotent small-time gangster
(Popeye); a cowardly and drunk-besotted student (Gowan);
a minor-league bootlegger (Goodwin); a former prostitute
(Goodwin's woman) and a "fast" young girl (Temple); a
congenital idiot (Tommy); and, as catalytic agent, a hen-
pecked lawyer (Horace). We are all familiar with the suggestion that *Sanctuary* marks the appearance of Greek tragedy
in the mystery novel, but the tragedy, with its cruelty to
which even death cannot put an end, is much more of a
biblical nature.

It is thus a *sacred* spell Faulkner wants to cast over us,
and the methods—or, if you prefer, the tricks—by which he
exercises his magnetic power deserve a closer scrutiny. The
most common one consists in having the real order of events
reconstituted by (that is, in having the story told by) a spectator of the drama who is at first external and indifferent to it
but who quickly becomes immersed—and by the end of a
few pages, implicated—in these affairs that do not in any way
concern him.

This is what happens to Horace Benbow in *Sanctuary*
(he becomes Goodwin's lawyer and is involuntarily responsible for the latter's convinction and lynching), and to the
nameless reporter of *Pylon*, who is fascinated by the strange
ménage à trois of Roger, Laverne, and the parachutist and
becomes so involved with them that he finally borrows the
money with which to buy Schumann the defective "crate" in
which he will ultimately go to his death. Such is also the fate

of Shreve and Quentin in *Absalom, Absalom!* Caught up in events they necessarily learn about differently (they cannot intervene in the action since everything has already irrevocably happened and all the dramatis personae are dead), they are nevertheless far removed from the cold objectivity of the perfect journalist, since (for Quentin, at least) it is to some extent their own futures that they are reading in the tragic fates of Sutpen, Henry, or Charles Bon.

We are also reminded of those innocents peacefully fishing at the lake of Galilee, Thomas Didymus and Simon Peter, or the sons of Zebadiah, who almost despite themselves become the witnesses, the *martyrs*, of an extraordinary Event. In nearly all of Faulkner's stories one finds (sometimes modestly hidden in a corner) a Witness, making things happen (like Horace Benbow) or conducting an investigation (like Quentin),[10] involved in but not necessarily understanding much about these affairs that do not concern him but from which he is incapable of freeing himself. A very curious ex-

---

[10] Whence springs Faulkner's almost perverse predilection for sinister stories told to children—for example, "A Justice" and "Red Leaves," which have to do with what might be called the "Indian prehistory" of Yoknapatawpha County and which old servants of the plantation tell in front of Quentin, who is all the more fascinated because he does not quite understand them. Like the character in another story, "Mistral," who cries on learning the truth about Evelyn Nesbitt, heroine of a famous *crime passionel*, "because Evelyn, who was a word, was beautiful and lost or I would never have heard of her," Quentin knows very well that he will not understand until it is too late. "We went on, in that strange faintly sinister suspension of twilight in which I believed that I could still see Sam Fathers back there, sitting on his wooden block, definite, immobile, and complete, like something looked upon after a long time in a preservative bath in a museum. That was it. I was just twelve then, and I would have to wait until I had passed on and through and beyond the suspension of twilight. Then I knew that I would know. But then Sam Fathers would be dead." [William Faulkner, "A Justice," *The Portable Faulkner*, New York, Viking, 1945, p. 45.]

ample of this is the unexpected introduction (at the end of the Appendix about the Compsons Faulkner added to the Viking Portable edition of his work) of a character never before mentioned—the old Jefferson librarian who discovers in 1943, in a French newspaper published during the Occupation, a photograph in which her old schoolfriend "Caddy" (sister of Jason, Quentin, and Benjy), as beautiful and young-looking as ever, is standing next to a sportscar and a German general in uniform. Neither Caddy's brother Jason, nor Dilsey, the old black nurse who was the Compsons' guardian angel, accepts the identification—which neither the old librarian nor the reader has any doubt about. Eyewitnesses risk being disbelieved when the things they reveal are too scandalous. But what is important is the kind of fascination the discovery has for the librarian. After a week of agitation that approaches madness, she abruptly leaves her library in the middle of the afternoon and enters, cheeks aflame with emotion, the dark shop in which the last of the Compsons sells to black farmers those items they cannot do without.

This emotion that so brusquely seizes upon the respectable old spinster is probably the same one that Faulkner feels each time he thinks of one of the beautiful and damned[11] characters that inhabit him; he most likely does not feel that he has created them any more than the librarian has begotten the photograph of a collaborationist Caddy. And if the situation of the "involved witness" is so important in his novels, it is because that is also precisely the situation of the reader of these novels.

We can no more free ourselves from the fascination Faulkner's characters exercise on us than they themselves can stop contemplating their fate. True, this attraction is mixed

[11] "Beautiful and lost," "Beautiful and damned," are the epithets he uses whenever he writes of Evelyn Nesbitt or Candace (Caddy) Compson.

with horror, like the feeling the bird has for the snake: in *Pylon*, the Reporter tortures himself with what could be called voyeuristic imaginings of the relationship between Laverne and the two men. It is as if sanctuaries, in Faulkner's world, take on their sacred character only with the profanation that deflowers them forever—as witness this long and astonishing sentence from *Absalom, Absalom!* in which the novelist sums up the essence of the ritual incest that implacably cements the trio of Henry, Judith, and Charles:

> In fact, perhaps this is the pure and perfect incest: the brother realizing that the sister's virginity must be destroyed in order to have existed at all, taking that virginity in the person of the brother-in-law, the man whom he would be if he could become, metamorphose into, the lover, the husband; by whom he would be despoiled, choose for despoiler, if he could become, metamorphose into the sister, the mistress, the bride.[12]

Temple's wait in Goodwin's house is prayer and contemplation as much as anguish; she seems to withdraw into herself to prepare for a consecration, as is demonstrated by the hieratic character of her positions:

> . . . in the silence Tommy could hear a faint, steady chatter of the shucks inside the mattress where Temple lay, her hands crossed on her breast and her legs straight and close and decorous, like an effigy on an ancient tomb.[13]

In the irrevocable, infinitely long-drawn-out moment before the profanation, the Sanctuary awaits the violating act that will make it forever a sanctuary. And of course, as Sartre has said with his usual good sense, "These enchantments are not possible. Not even conceivable." We are right in the middle of the "black novel," and any page of *Absalom, Absalom!* or of *Sanctuary* seems as if it might have been torn out from

[12] William Faulkner, *Absalom, Absalom!*, p. 96.—Tr.
[13] William Faulkner, *Sanctuary*, p. 42.—Tr.

Sade's *Les Cent Vingt Journées* (*The Hundred and Twenty Days of Sodom*) or *La Nouvelle Justine.* Faulkner pretends to give us exact descriptions of everyday life no more than Sade did; but the world of enchantments is not less *real* than the other, and in any case it is in complete harmony with the very special structure of the universe that the novelist is committed to present to us.

Maurice Blanchot, in an admirably perceptive observation on the epithets of Julien Gracq,[14] notes that the use of adjectives—which traditional rhetoricians advise against on the grounds that they overload the language and make it heavy and slow—can nevertheless be justified if the writer (for whatever personal reason) has to seem to write badly and wants purposely to encumber the overdirect paths opened through the world by his style—in other words, if he has to again entrammel the words that speech makes too fluid at every moment, to entrammel himself in them, and us, the readers, as well. This is exactly what Faulkner does when he entwines three, four, or five adjectives around one unfortunate noun.[15] One can apply to his style, word for word, what Blanchot said of the style of Gracq's *Un Beau ténébreux* (*A Dark Stranger*): because of this thickening of the language by means of the superabundance of adjectives, we end by *seeing* much less distinctly those things that the author believes himself to be describing, but we *feel* them better. What the author is consequently able to give us "is an indistinct whole, a world of things that either are unorganized or are in the process of becoming disorganized, where there is no longer either a classification to make or a perspective to draw"—a definition that perfectly fits the Faulknerian *glue* in which we are caught.

[14] *Les Cahiérs de la Pléiade* (2).

[15] See, for example, the second line of *Absalom, Absalom!* previously cited: "the long still hot weary dead September afternoon . . ."

"There are no adjectives in nature," Claude Roy very justly observes in his *Description critique* devoted to Colette (that other specialist of three adjectives). This is because qualifiers (so inoffensive on the surface) are so many magic means by which man can appropriate nature. Far from *describing* things, as common sense naïvely believes (such description would mean literally to reproduce by language, to *mime*, already existing characteristics), these qualifiers mark our power over things, things that are re-created by us in our image, things that are given particularities that make no sense except in relation to us. An adjective is not a photograph or a mold; it cannot in any way claim to explain the essence of something (a role semantics reserves to the substantive). A beach is not in itself "desolate" (as in Gracq), or a September afternoon "weary" (or "dead" or "long")—except through the intermediary of a human consciousness. Even the fact that something is red or blue implies at least the presence of a retina. To charge "things" with more "qualities" than current language can bear is simply to provide them with so many *handles* by which we can, when we wish, catch them, control them, make them serve our own ends. It is obvious that a certain kind of writer might use epithets to present things to the reader in a magical way, to *suggest* them rather than truly to describe them—in short, *to force them to appear*, which is the strict meaning of the word "evoke."

As Blanchot so well reminds us, "In magic, things try to exist in the manner of consciousness, and consciousness is closer to the existence of things." Now, when we lose ourselves in Faulkner's long sentences, heavy with adjectives and incidents, we get bogged down in them, we literally get *entrammeled*. Our consciousness, which congeals and becomes more obscure, tends toward the opaque, blind, and totally self-oriented mode of existence, which is doubtless that of the inorganic, of the thing, while, correlatively, objects begin to live and become charged with the intentions and qualities previously reserved to men: the afternoon becomes weary or the beach desolate, while the violated young girl becomes a sanctuary and characters become "thingified," immobilized in the contemplation of the overwhelming past.[16]

To use Sartre's language, the *"en-soi"* and the *"pour-soi"* exchange their characteristics in Faulkner: men become as much as possible like things, stubborn and inert, while by means of epithets things become subtly alive, as if they could perceive and be aware. In "Old Man," the tale that makes up half of *The Wild Palms*, the overflowing Mississippi possesses a more powerful reality than does the long-time prisoner, the involuntary escapee, who is the story's protagonist. In "A Justice" and "Red Leaves," the shoes with red heels brought from Paris by "The Man" Issetibbeha, which are symbols of his hereditary power (and which are actually too small for either himself or his obese son Moketubbe), have a stronger existence than the colorless consciousness of the two men. In the same way, in the story "Hair" (in the collection *These Thirteen*) the true heroine is not young Susan Burchett, a small, thin girl with neither beauty nor personality, but her strange, straight silky hair, neither blonde nor brown, which is the only thing in the world the hairdresser Hawkshaw loves (because it reminds him of the hair of his dead fiancée, and which is the reason he marries the girl despite the difference in their ages and the shamelessness of her life). The most striking example of this technique is perhaps to be found in

[16] Jean Pouillon quite subtly notes that Joe Christmas's black blood (in *Light in August*) has no objective truth and rests "in the final analysis on gossip and the beliefs of an old woman." In his comments on *Sartoris*, Sartre rightly insists on the aspect of *idols*—blind and mute—that Faulkner has succeeded in conferring on his characters thanks to procedures Sartre condemns as specious, such as that of never showing us the consciousness of characters except when they are emptied of themselves in action or sleep.

Pylon, a novel completely dedicated to the description of the fascination exercised on men by the machine, and in which the planes and the pilots—the former so much more real than the latter—seem to have exchanged their qualities, as the Reporter tells the editor of his paper.[17] Like his witness, like his reader, Faulkner is hallucinated by this spectacle of an inhuman humanity that might just as well have gas instead of blood in its veins.

The examples could be multiplied. The important thing is the meaning of this magical exchange, in the heart of the novel, between beings and things, and the profound necessity for it. In a work of imagination, neither objects nor events nor anything else that belongs to the material world and has just been torn from it ever appears as it is. The absolute impossibility of incorporating such elements into the web of the story seems quite obvious as soon as we think about it (though here, as elsewhere, we must first begin by fooling ourselves, and the only truths that are really acquired have had to be paid for a hundred times over with error and foolishness). Mallarmé formulated this with his habitual acuity (he, also, after having undoubtedly paid the necessary ransom of stupidity and dearly discharged his debts for the liquidation of the ambition that inspired his supreme works) in a famous passage from his *Divagations*:

> We renounce that erroneous aesthetic (even though it has been responsible for certain masterpieces) which would have the poet fill the delicate pages of his book with the actual and palpable wood of trees, rather than with the forest's

[17] ". . . they ain't human like us; they couldn't turn those pylons like they do if they had human blood and senses and they wouldn't want to or dare to if they just had human brains. Burn them like this one tonight and they don't even holler in the fire; crash one and it ain't even blood when you haul him out: it's cylinder oil the same as in the crankcase." [William Faulkner, *Pylon,* p. 45.]

shuddering or the silent scattering of thunder through the foliage.[18]

This idea, when applied to the novel, signifies that neither the concrete object nor the temporal act can figure in it. All that can be included on "the delicate pages of the book" and communicated to the reader is their human significance —that is, the impression they have produced, the emotion they have given rise to, hypothetically in the imaginary protagonists of the story, very definitely in the author who has created them and who cannot pretend to be communicating anything other than this sense, this emotion: in short, the contents of his own consciousness at the moment of imagining.

The abuse of epithets is one of the multiple instruments of the special sorcery of every great writer, by means of which, as Malraux says in his preface to the French translation of *Sanctuary*,[19] he incorporates his private obsession into the web of the universe, thus seeking to free himself of it by projecting it onto the object—and, I will add, by forcing us to share it. It is significant that Malraux, whose particular obsession is a sharp sense of the absolute noncommunication between beings, should have seen only the relationship of the work of art to the world, ignoring the no less essential bond that unites it to the public that will be the *consumer*. And yet everyone knows that he who has sold his soul to the devil cannot liberate himself except by finding a new and voluntary victim who will be his substitute in the execution of the pact.

---

[18] Stéphane Mallarmé, "Crisis in Poetry," in *Mallarmé: Selected Prose Poems, Essays, and Letters*, trans. by Bradford Cook, Baltimore, Johns Hopkins Press, 1956, p. 40.—Tr.

[19] "The tragic poet expresses what fascinates him—not to deliver himself of it (the object of his fascination will reappear in his next work) but to change its nature. . . . He does not defend himself against anguish by expressing it, but by expressing something else with it, by reintroducing it into the universe. . . ."

Only on this condition will Melmoth be reconciled or the genii of the bottle appeased.

It is no different in art: the sorcerer cannot be freed unless he succeeds in enchanting in his turn. Consequently, no one reads a great book with impunity; readers of Dostoevski, Malraux, Faulkner, quickly become their accomplices—also, I fear, their substitutes. The arts in their turn may also some day be considered a form of crime. And each writer must invent his own means of achieving the adhesion of the reader, at least to such a point that he can obtain from him the voluntary sacrifice that will be his own salvation.

Literature as a Sacrifice of Substitutions

Jean Prévost judiciously observes that the particular charm of *La Chartreuse de Parme* is due to the very rapidity with which it was written—twenty or thirty pages a day, dictated over a period of fifty-one days without a break. This is because, he says, the improviser "conceives while he writes, identifies himself with his characters: the inventive impulse of the author is the same as the passionate impulse of the hero, and the sympathetic impulse of the reader"—so much so that "while reading, we feel ourselves living with the hero and creating with the author."[20] One could generalize from this statement and say that every fully successful novel is so by virtue of this identification that it is able to produce, through the agency of the characters of the story, between the writer and his reader—an identification, however, capable of being effected by means quite different from the creative vivacity we feel in *La Chartreuse*.[21]

[20] Jean Prévost, *La Création chez Stendhal*, Editions du Sagittaire.
[21] One could further extend the remark by applying it to poems. I have elsewhere tried to show how Mallarmé went about the task of making the reader identify with him and truly become the *author* of what he is reading.

Thus, in Balzac, it is the intensity of the novelistic vision itself that is communicated to us, bringing us face to face with characters who, no matter how schematic or unreal they may be, exist more forcefully than do people in everyday life—which even Henry James, whose art is at the antipodes of that of the father of the illustrious Gaudissart, had to recognize. I have elsewhere used, in connection with Giraudoux, the words "novelistic aplomb" to describe the calm audacity with which he brings forth propositions like: "From 1914 to 1918 German women cuckolded their husbands barely more than usual, collectors of libertine novels bought very little more than usual, writers did not commit suicide at all"— statements certainly impossible to prove in any of the usual ways, yet perfectly admissible because they simply signify that we have left the ordinary world and entered a universe of incorruptible essences, where the novelist is as omnipotent and omniscient as God the Father. Balzaeian "hustling" (which James compares to that of a traveling saleman praising his merchandise or to a magician sure of succeeding with his marked cards) and Faulknerian "sorcery" are just two means of forcing the reader to accomplish *himself* this "sacrifice of substitution," which is without doubt the very essence of literature and without which a work is nothing more than a succession of vain words set down on paper.

This concept leads quite naturally to the idea of art having an almost sacred function, a role it probably inherits from that previously assumed to a large extent by religion. But I would like to keep to a consideration of Faulkner and show how sacrifice is consummated in his work.

I have already noted—as have many others before me—that even when the story begins in an impersonal mode, we are soon being shown its events through the eyes of a witness, who is at first only responsible for the particular point of view of the narration, but who is quickly caught up by what he sees and soon engaged in the action. (Thus, the Reporter in *Pylon* and the lawyer Benbow in *Sanctuary* are ultimately responsible for the final catastrophe.) The frequency of this procedure can of course be explained by a scruple of artistic honesty, the concern to point out that a narrative is always the narrative of *someone*, that an event, to be apprehended— that is, to *be*—must be perceived by a consciousness. But such idealism is a bit surprising in Faulkner—whom, by the way, Sartre accused, not too unjustly, of "dishonesty"[22] (when he was discussing, it is true, one of his unsuccessful stories, in which art is often no more than artifice).

It should also be noted that Faulkner's Witness never remains neutral or indifferent for very long, which is quite different from what happens in Henry James, whose art might quite often be described as the art of a "voyeur." I see this gradually bewitched man, whom the writer interposes between us, the reader, and his creation, as an intermediary —and even as a Mediator—with whom, as the story progresses, we identify to such an extent that our vision more and more coincides with his, and who gradually introduces us, by means of imperceptible transitions, to the very heart of the author's personal universe—which seemed, at the beginning, as if it would remain irremediably incommunicable.

T. S. Eliot says in a note to *The Waste Land* that "what Tiresias *sees*" constitutes the very texture of his poem. In the same way it can be said that to the extent that what Faulkner has wanted and seen becomes the very texture of the consciousness of Horace Benbow or the Reporter (or of Quentin and Shreve in *Absalom, Absalom!*), this content of consciousness passes into the imagination of the reader as if through the locks of a sluice. As a result, we become not only this or

[22] "So much art and, to tell the truth, so much dishonesty, are merely attempts to replace intuition of the future, intuition the author lacks . . ." (*Situations*, I, p. 78).

that particular character—Temple, Popeye, or Goodwin's woman, or Schumann, Laverne, Jiggs—but the total reality that they form (exactly as in *The Waste Land* we are equally Cleopatra, the stenographer, Mr. Eugenides, the fortune teller, Philomela; or, in Joyce's *Ulysses*, Bloom, Stephen Daedalus, Gertie McDowell, the two hotel barmaids).

Whence the importance of *fascination* in this work of double transmission? Faulkner begins by communicating his own obsession to his creations: he makes them react to the particular spectacles to which they are witnesses with the same mixture of horror and attraction that he experiences when faced with the world in general. This is how the Reporter feels when faced with the trio of Laverne and the two men, and with the strange (to him) world of aviators; how Benbow feels faced with Goodwin and his gang; Quentin and Shreve, with Sutpen's behavior; and, to a lesser degree, young Quentin, with the prehistoric world of the Indians in two of the stories in *These Thirteen*.

On the one hand, the author objectifies his fascination in a spectacle, projects his emotion outside himself by supposing for it an imaginary origin, a counterpart external to himself —what T. S. Eliot called the "objective correlative." But this "objective correlative" (that is, the structure of his stories, the plot) is not the only thing he counts on to set off in us the same emotion or to obtain our participation: the Witnesses, the Mediators, are charged with the task of communicating to us, by a kind of contagion, what they feel.[23] It is because

23 It should also be noted that sometimes, in a kind of rebound this "fascination" reacts on the plot and modifies it, as if to further increase the horror of the story. The archetype of this is the end of *Sanctuary*, where Goodwin, terrorized by Popeye, is obsessed on the eve of his judgment by the idea that Popeye will come to the jail and assassinate him, which turns the attention of Lee and Benbow from the dramatic event which is being prepared behind the scenes and precipitates the catastrophe.

they are fascinated that we will see with their eyes and be fascinated in turn. In the same way, in *La Chartreuse de Parme*, Stendhal's feelings of quasi-paternal tenderness and extreme indulgence for Fabrice, the son he never had, is so directly communicated to us that we are blinded to the character's real mediocrity (at least until he falls hopelessly in love with Clélia); Saint-Beuve noted this, and it becomes quite obvious as soon as one thinks about it. This is a good example of how the novelist enchants the reader. In this case it is Stendhal's blindness vis-à-vis his spiritual son that is transmitted to us, partly directly and partly through the tenderness that Mosca and the Duchess feel for Fabrice.

But Faulkner has still other ways besides his use of epithets and his recourse to Mediators by which to work his enchantments; and most of the difficulties in his work, his apparent perversities, can be explained by this ambition to achieve a *total* identification between the writer and his reader. A simple and shocking example of this is the homonymy between different characters in the same story, for example, the two Quentins (uncle and niece) in *The Sound and the Fury*.[24] (Incidentally, in this novel Faulkner has not yet begun to use the technique of the Witness-Mediator, and he gives us the various components of his vision "in separate parts" [as he had previously done in *While I Lay Dying*], leaving us the task of linking them to make a total picture—which is perhaps too much to ask of the reader. Subsequent works testify to a certain progress.) The recurrence of Quentin's name in the story poses no problem of ambiguity for the author, who holds all the strings and is always quite certain as to whether he means the uncle or the niece without

[24] Also in *The Sound and the Fury*, the two Jasons (father and son) and in *Sanctuary* the two Belles (Horace's wife and the daughter of her first marriage), but these ambiguities recur less frequently and are much less disturbing to the reader.

ever having to think about it. The extra effort of reflection and
attention we must make in order to discriminate between
them forces us to pass through to the other side of the carpet
—to the side where he, the author, is busy knotting the
threads of his plot; it *obliges* us to adopt his point of view—
that of immediate and unambiguous knowledge, that of the
creative vision. If he is sometimes deliberately obscure, it is
never because of disdain for the reader; on the contrary, his
enigmas are so many means of assuring our complicity. *In a
word, thanks to them he forces us to put ourselves in his place,
to become the authors of what we are reading.*

The essayist and the poet—Alain or Paulhan, Rimbaud
or Mallarmé—do not behave any differently when they deliberately delay the communication of a meaning (which ultimately they wish understood) by obscuring it in various
ways. If their meaning were transmitted too easily, if it were
not paid for by our efforts, it would quickly be forgotten. We
can here see the birth of the idea of a truly "Marxist" and
cooperative literature, in which no one will be able to be a
consumer if he is not willing at the same time to be a producer. This means that the work—essay, novel, or poem—to
be truly profitable to the one who reads it, must cease being
something unjustly acquired as a finished product—prepared
in advance, consumed as it is, and completely exhausted in
this one absorption; it must instead become an ambiguous,
unfinished object that requires, to fully *be*, the cooperation of
the reader, who assumes the responsibility for a part of its
creation.

The ideal of this art would thus be to transform the work
into a kind of *trap*, in which the reader would be forced, like
a squirrel in a wheel, into a mechanism that would function,
because of his own efforts, from the moment in which he steps
into it—that is, from the time when, having begun to read
novel, poem, or essay, he feels himself put on his mettle by

their apparent impenetrability and can have no rest until he successfully concludes the work to which the author has merely *incited* him. A page of prose, for example, might be nothing more than a series of notations without any apparent logical connection other than what the reader himself would be forced—morally, of course—to invent. (A description that seems to apply quite well to Paulhan's essays, and certainly to Alain's *propos*.) The point would be not so much to communicate a preexistent meaning—known to the author from the beginning, but spitefully hidden from us out of coquetry or sadism—as to force the reader to look behind the words to the hidden, more profound meaning that is nowhere expressly embodied in the writing. This would satisfy what must be every writer's secret ambition: to be indefinitely multiplied, to exist in as many versions as there are *true* readers, to create a theoretically limitless number of beings similar to himself.

Faulkner's great originality is to have succeeded in bringing that notoriously lazy being, the reader of novels, under this hard and truly Socratic discipline. (Balzac, Meredith, Melville, Henry James, to say nothing of Stendhal, had, of course, already labored to some purpose in this area.) He is thus able to evade what seems as if it must be one of his major difficulties, one related to the very essence of his message: the problem of suggesting by means of narrative art, which is based on connections—whether temporal or causal is of no importance—the idea that we live in an absurd world. By its very nature, even the most disordered, chaotic narration cannot help but introduce into the events it reports an excess of order, which overelucidates and overillumines those events. Such is the ransom all the discursive arts pay to the instrument they use. Even the most ordinary prose necessarily says more than it should, and tends to deprive thought of that part of the indispensable shadow without which there is no light, and reason of the element of madness without which, as Paulhan has so well shown,[25] there is no wisdom.

It is difficult for the storyteller not to strip his narrative of this novelistic opacity without which it becomes light and thin (this happened quite often in Stendhal, and this was perhaps his only weakness). He can only maintain this opacity by an obstinate determination, by a constantly renewed vow never to transfigure the story by the intelligence of the narrator, no matter how acute it may be. This enables us to understand why Faulkner, when he was still only testing himself in his art, armed himself against this kind of temptation by consigning the first part of *The Sound and the Fury*'s narration to the idiot Benjy (which is reminiscent of the story of the painter who so hated the pretty and so feared his own facility that for years he forced himself to use only his left hand). The events narrated in this fashion retain for the rest of the novel an inkiness that nothing can remove, that is rediscovered on each new reading. In later works the novelist has become more subtle, and he makes us uncover the facts pellmell, following in the footsteps of a witness as ignorant, as intrigued as ourselves.

Balzac provides as many examples of chronological displacements as Faulkner, though they are less evident because of their very variety. Examples include *La Duchesse de Langeais*, which begins with the denouement and goes back into the past; or the two interwoven stories, one taking place in the present and under our eyes, the other quite old and forgotten, that constitute *L'Auberge rouge* (*The Red House*); or the sudden accelerations in the tempo of a story, as in the end of *La Muse du départément* (*The Muse of the Department*) from the moment when Diane has resolved to

[25] A little in all his work, and especially in *Entretiens sur les faits divers*.

leave Lousteau; or the many abrupt denouements that so frequently contrast with the long, almost interminable, preparations of the beginnings. It is this variety that makes them so
instructive. They do not have the obsessional quality of
Faulkner's monotonous orientation of time to the past; they
have no other visible function but to keep reality from being
attenuated and eroded by the very means used to describe
it—discursive narration, which is necessarily analytical. Because of these displacements, events recover the original
density of chaos.

For Faulkner, negation is one of the major means of preserving this matrix of darkness necessary to his art. To take its
simplest form first, this consists of the almost simplistic method
of restoring to an event its "shadowy side"—without which it
could not be completely real—by not telling us everything,
by leaving precisely what is essential in the shadows. In Pierre
Benoit this method is caricatured in advance and transformed
into a narrator's tic as devoid of true significance as the one
that gives all the heroines names beginning with "A"; in
Faulkner, however, the fact that the crucial moments are
hidden from view is the result of many factors and charged
with diverse meanings, the multiplicity of which is exactly
what keeps it from being a simple artifice. Its function is not
only to disconcert us or to assure our complicity in the quest
and thus involve us in the action, or even simply to suggest
that the past is the only reality and the event itself nothing,
because it is only known too late—in other words, "thingified,"
made similar to things, "unrealized," in other words, absent,
become imaginary: it is meant to signify all of this at one
time and we are the more inclined to accept these various
ideas because Faulkner has not imposed them but has led us
to formulate them ourselves.

A superior sorcerer, Faulkner even renounces enchanting
us directly; he limits himself to putting within our reach (as

one leaves a gun near a doomed man so that he may kill himself) the necessary instruments for giving birth to the obscure fascination he wants to induce and for producing in us the desire to undergo such anguish. Ultimately, as the ones solely responsible for these enchantments, we will find in his work only what we have agreed to put into it.

Rivalry with God the Father—Faulkner and Balzac

Faulkner easily confuses reader and critic alike by the unusual and strange progression of his narrative. To accustom oneself to it, to see what is happening behind its astonishing façade, one must have both a long familiarity with the work (only possible through frequent rereadings) and the ability to stand back from the individual narrative thread of *one* story in order to see all of them adding to each other and merging with each other like fragments of a single great work.[26]

For example, I do not think enough attention has been paid to the fact that there is in Faulkner, as there is in Balzac, a reappearance of characters and a consequent interweaving of story with story. Before *Sanctuary*, Horace Benbow had

[26] We should carefully note, in what follows, that with Faulkner as with Balzac, the dates of composition do not always coincide with those of publication—especially when it is a question of collections of stories in which we sometimes cannot date any given one. For example, we know that Balzac wrote *Une Double Famille* (*A Second Family*) over a twelve-year period and that he deliberated over *César Birotteau* for eight years before deciding to get it down on paper. In the same way, though Faulkner published *Sartoris* in 1929 and *The Sound and The Fury* six months later, the latter was the one written first. "Wash," published in 1934 in the collection *Doctor Martino*, was written at the same time as the stories of *The Hamlet*. This observation merely confirms the hypothesis of a simultaneity of vision that precedes, in Balzac as in Faulkner, the actual transcription of the work.

already appeared in *Sartoris*, as had his aunt Miss Jenny, the heroine of "There Was a Queen." The story of *Absalom, Absalom!*, that obscure and complex tale of incest *à trois*, is told by a spinster lady to Quentin Compson, who is the hero of *The Sound and the Fury* and who commits suicide because of his love for his sister, whom Benjy, the family idiot, also loves passionately. In the course of this story, we meet the Sutpens, a dynasty whose tragic end has already been told us in "Wash," one of the stories originally published in the collection *Doctor Martino and Other Stories*. The same holds true for Faulkner's later books: we again meet the Sartorises (as well as the Snopeses of *Sanctuary*) in *The Unvanquished*, and certain minor characters of *As I Lay Dying* reappear in *The Hamlet*.

All this suggests the idea of a *total* world, one that can hardly be guessed at and certainly not understand if we are only familiar with two or three of its parts—a world that seems to have existed fully, from its inception, in the mind of the author, who thus finds himself placed (involuntarily and probably unconsciously) on *the right side* of this world—on "the good side" of it—while we, alas, see only the wrong side of the carpet. This is true but unfortunate, since the author is unaware of this; so absorbed is he in his vision, so completely involved in the effort to bring it forth, that he can spare no time to put it right side up for us and make it intelligible.

This is undoubtedly another explanation for Faulkner's seeming indifference—distraction rather than contempt—to the public: his eyes are so fixed on the universe within him that he comes to believe that everything is as clear to us as it is to him, and he never ceases to treat the eventual reader like another self. This explains the extraordinary, and certainly unplanned, two-page addendum to Caddy's biography at the end of the previously mentioned *Portable Faulkner*. Like Balzac, Faulkner keeps forgetting that it is sometimes necessary to please. Immured in the total solitude of the creator, he no longer thinks in terms of an ultimate public, real or fictitious, actual or potential; he has enough to do in unraveling the complex web formed by the strands that link his characters.

Actually, this creative indifference (once the intial annoyance it necessarily causes is surmounted) adds to the *impressive* quality of the work, which towers over us, in all its massiveness, like a section of a cyclopean wall. This work certainly preexists our reading, and we are almost tempted to say that it even preexists its author and his transcription of it. It demands nothing of us, neither respect nor admiration, nor does it flatter us or hope to seduce us: its mere existence is enough to attract our attention. Like the Civil War, like the important shadowy events it invites us to contemplate from afar (instead of describing them to us), it is there before us, an immobile image of eternity offered to our attention—and consequently the exact opposite of the Time that presides over the revolutions of the cosmos, which Plato defined so well in *Timaeus* as "a mobile image of eternity."

Faulkner's short stories are, like Balzac's, microcosms; each of them reflects the whole of the work just as the Leibnizian monad reflects the universe. Pick up at random "That Evening Sun" or "Wash," and you will find all the familiar themes. First there is the theme of the magic force of destiny, manifested by the black woman Nancy sitting by the fire and waiting as if hypnotized for the husband she knows is going to kill her—nothing in the world having the power to stop him. In the second story the theme is embodied by Sutpen, who *purposely gets himself killed* by Wash Jones, with that frightening precipitation that makes Faulkner's characters not only "run to meet their destiny" (as we feebly put it) but actually impale themselves on it. Then there is the theme of the witness, as "innocent" as he is powerless. For

Nancy, the witnesses are the Compson children, who are so hypnotized by the resignation of the Negro woman sitting by the fire that she is *already* dead for them ("Who's going to wash our clothes now Daddy?" says Quentin, long before the murder has taken place and even before the arrival of the murderer).

Other themes are the dismissal of the event, already driven into the past as much by the protagonists as by the spectators (the chorus of the Compson children) even before it has happened; and—the immediate consequence of this for the narration—the author's concealment of what really happened, the hiding of the event at the moment it actually occurs and the deferred communication of its effect to a later part of the work, where it is usually limited to an almost unnoticed parenthetical remark in a context where our attention is focused on other characters. Each of Faulkner's narratives is like a piece of one enormous puzzle, making sense only as part of the whole.

This "whole" is materialized in a Faulknerian geography that is as objective as the map of France in *La Comédie humaine.* Indeed, it is in precisely the form of a map placed at the beginning of *The Portable Faulkner.* Malcolm Cowley, in his Introduction to this edition, perceives the principle of this metaphysical analogy—pregnant with innumerable aesthetic consequences—that I have tried to elucidate: all the stories that refer to the Yoknapatawpha saga (that being the name of *terra faulkneriana,* the new kingdom discovered by Faulkner) are part of one living reality; and it is this reality, rather than the actual printed volumes, in which only part of it is transcribed, that constitutes Faulkner's true literary work. It is the objective (in the most precise sense of this term) existence of this country that gives each of Faulkner's stories, long or short, its extraordinary power of suggestion and sense of reality—and, incidentally, it also explains why Faulkner should be so incapable of telling the same story twice without adding new details, as is proved by the Compson biography that ends the volume.[27] This is only proper for a writer who each time that he thinks again of one of his imaginary creations finds himself confronting the totality of his vision, as if face to face with the God he has been in all but actuality.

Balzac did the same. With his famous "trick" of having characters reappear, he invented *the* archetypal means of enabling the reader to participate in the privileged situation of the novelist as creator rather than as visionary. In *Balzac romancier* Maurice Bardéche has enumerated some of the most striking literary results of this procedure (whatever may have been the author's original reasons for employing it). He especially insists on the striking impression of reality that is produced, as much in the story itself as in the objective existence of characters who for the first time seem endowed with the "third dimension," which did not again appear until Proust:

> Balzac creates out of whole cloth a sort of Romantic perspective by means which are peculiar to him, giving a future or a continuous present to stories which he relates, and making his imaginary characters, characters which belong to us as well as to him and whose witnesses we become.[28]

The credibility of Balzac's characters is thereby strongly augmented. Paradoxically, the novelist manages to make them exist more strongly by the "blanks" in their existence than by the parts that are filled in, by what we do not know about them more than by what is told us, just as in Faulkner the intensity of events is felt in proportion to the degree of care taken to

[27] See Malcolm Cowley's Introduction to *The Portable Faulkner*, pp. 8–9.

[28] Quoted from Maurice Bardèche, *Balzac romancier*, in Philippe Bertault, *Balzac and the Human Comedy*, trans. by Richard Monges, New York, New York University Press, 1965, p. 134.—Tr.

hide them from us. We actually know very little about characters like de Marsay and La Palférine—or about Vautrin's past—and yet they exist in such strikingly strong relief! Painting needs shadow no less than light, and as Sartre says about Faulkner: "Divination makes magical what it touches." When a novelist uses characters that are already familiar to the reader, he is able to combine the precision one has the right to expect of a portrayal with the "unfinished" quality indispensable for it to be fully evocative.

I have already cited numerous examples of this "reappearance" of characters in Faulkner; there are, of course, others.[29] Thus, in *Sartoris*, the first of the books published by Faulkner, in Spring, 1929, we see Byron Snopes steal a packet of letters from Narcissa Benbow (who will reappear in *Sanctuary*, published in 1931). Only in "There Was a Queen," a story published five years later, do we find out how Narcissa went about getting her letters back. Or again, in the first

[29] We must, however, note that in Faulkner as in Balzac the method has a disadvantage: it results in slight variations or incoherencies (whichever you prefer) in the presentation of a character. But this is almost always limited to details, and is of minor importance: the house Sutpen builds of bricks at the beginning of *Absalom, Absalom!* catches fire at the end of the novel, being by that time made of wood and completely flammable except for the chimneys; the sewing machine salesman named Ratliffe in *The Hamlet* is called V. K. Suratt in *Sartoris* and several of the stories; Henry Armstrong's wife is sometimes named Martha, sometimes Lula. It is as difficult to take these inconsistencies seriously as it is to be concerned about the fact that Balzac's heroines' eyes change color. I find the *essential* coherence of Balzac and Faulkner remarkable, especially given the large scale of their work and the long time span of the composition. Think, for example, of the perfect cohesion of Balzac's biography of l'Abbé Birrotteau (the "Curé de Tours" and brother of the perfumer), which has been carefully examined by Philippe Bertault in his book *Balzac: L'Homme et l'oeuvre* (Boivin). This is because only such information as is basic to the character of the hero is given. Faulkner, so far as I know, has never gotten confused about the complex genealogy of his Sartorises, Compsons, or Sutpens, either.

chapter of *Sanctuary* there is an allusion to a hidden treasure buried during the Civil War (in exactly the spot where Popeye kills Tommy), which the people in the area occasionally dig for with "secret and sporadic optimism." The last chapter of *The Hamlet* gives us a picture of such a search. The most immediate effect of the method—which obviously presupposes a rather extensive degree of familiarity with Faulkner's work (though because of his good qualities as much as his faults he must surely be one of those rare novelists who has only serious readers)—is to extend the characters in depth, to give them a past—a "past definite," if one may put it that way, which casts the events being recounted into a far past whose limits we cannot see.

In this sense, their situation exactly reproduces that of Faulkner's entire universe, which is not only, as so often happens, a cut made into time, but which is exactly the opposite —an attempt to be the memory of a race and a country, of precisely *this* country whose secret sickness is the absence of roots and traditions.[30] While in *The Sound and the Fury* the present-tense time of the novel goes from 1910 to 1928, the Compson genealogy we find at the end of *The Portable Faulkner* goes back to the battle of Culloden in 1745 and forward to 1945. The whole of Faulkner's work could be considered a vast autobiography, not of a single individual but of a whole country, a whole bloc of humanity. And its secret charm (especially evident in *Absalom, Absalom!*) is undoubtedly that it gives evidence at every moment of that indispensable quality for successful memoirs which Charles du Bos, who regrets its absence in the first part of *Si le Grain ne meurt* (*If It Die . . .*), calls *afflux*: that gushing forth from artesian wells, that irresistible flow of inner sap which so quickly (as in Stendhal's *La Vie de Henri Brulard* [*The Life of Henry*

[30] See the concluding chapter.

Brulard]) sweeps away all the deliberate effects the author might originally have wanted to introduce into his act of recall—effects that can make the work (as happened in Rousseau's *Confessions*) pass into the realm of obvious self-justification and even of lies.

This invasion of the writer by what he calls forth, this overwhelming of him—and from all sides—by the things he merely wants to record (and which so deliciously submerge us when we read Henry James's admirable "Middle Years"[31] or the best pages of Proust) is what sweeps us up and carries us away in the best of Faulkner's works—like the tumultuous Mississippi that is the true hero of *The Wild Palms*. It is not the different depth-levels of an individual, hence limited, "I" coming to the surface, but a collective unconscious; and its reappearance in the light of day is accompanied by the same irresistible vertigo as greets the explorations of our own past by dream or analysis.

A writer so invaded and actually *possessed* by what he wants to say, will try, as best he can, to say everything at once. Faulkner's sentences—like Proust's, like Henry James's —are like webs, like nets thrown over a too-rich reality that the novelist has no right, lest he betray it, to analyze or sift. It is good that the reader feel himself, for a moment, trapped, entangled, submerged; that is how the author felt a moment earlier. For example, the beginning of *Sanctuary* is obscure largely because of Faulkner's effort to show us things all at once and exactly as they are seen by the various characters.

Just as Orson Welles reacted against the technique of cutting by juxtaposing both the foreground and the background in a single image, keeping both in sharp focus, so Faulkner reacts, by the complexity of his narration, against

---

[31] I am referring, of course, to the unfinished autobiographical fragment that follows *Notes of a Son and Brother*, and not to the story of the same name.

everything analytical and disassociative that is necessarily part of both narrative and speech—and he most likely does it quite deliberately, quite knowingly. He is trying to give us a vision not so much of an absurd world as of a universe in which everything coexists, in which all beings are simultaneously perceived. Thus, the interior monologue of the idiot Benjy is symbolic insofar as it momentarily restores to us an image of this synthesized universe—of the "whole of feeling," to use F. H. Bradley's expression—in which reality has not yet been defracted into a multiplicity of guises by the intervention of clear self-awareness.

Faulkner's aspiration toward synthesis explains the predominance, noted by almost all the critics, of plot over characterization, events over men. One could apply to him, almost word for word, what T. S. Eliot said about Henry James—that "compared with James's characters, other novelists' characters seem to be only accidentally in the same book," and that "the real hero, in any of James's stories, is a social entity of which men and women are constituent elements." And this is what Malraux says about *Sanctuary*:

> I would not be the slightest bit surprised to find that he often thought of his scenes before imagining his characters, that for him the work of art was not a story whose unfolding determines the tragic situations, but quite the opposite—that the story is born of the drama of the opposition or the destruction of unknown characters, and that imagination served only to lead these characters logically to the preconceived situation.

This conjecture is completely confirmed by empiric reality, since Maurice Coindreau tells us that the basic idea of *The Sound and the Fury* first imposed itself on the author as the portrayal of the reactions of a group of restless children.[32]

It is hardly possible to generalize on the basis of two

[32] Maurice Coindreau, *Aspects du roman américain*, Gallimard, p. 113.

examples (to which one would have to add that of Hawthorne and perhaps also that of Melville, more difficult to analyze) and claim that this subordination of individuals to the larger structure of the plot as a whole is a characteristic of the American novel. Yet we do find in Dos Passos and in O'Hara—otherwise so different from Hawthorne and Faulkner—the same kind of characters, overwhelmed, caught in an inexorable trap (whether economic, social, or hereditary is of no importance), and having little more real existence or liberty than a pawn in a chess game. It is in any case obvious that the psychological or biographical particularities of Faulkner's characters are strictly determined by the necessities of the plot—what Malraux calls the machine for "crushing man." In *Sanctuary*, Temple must be exactly what she is in order to cause the downfall of the innocent Goodwin by bearing false witness against him. In *The Wild Palms*, the unsuccessful abortion (with which the story begins) is of prime importance: it shapes the character of both the doctor and Charlotte, and governs the different facets of their life together; no element has any other function, any other reason for existence, than to converge toward this inexorable catastrophe.

It often happens that the Faulknerian character, instead of being defined in the usual way by a collection of psychological, biographical, and social particularities, which taken together give him his individuality, has a structure defined by one single, timeless, immutable act—which does not have to be spectacular and which even, since it is situated outside of time, often so far back in the past that it has become unreal and indistinguishable from legend, does not have to have really happened. This is true of Christmas's black blood, of the crime committed long ago by the convict in *The Wild Palms*, and of Popeye's pointless cruelty. The essence of Lena Grove, at the beginning of *Light in August*, is to walk, to walk, to walk endlessly, lured on by a hope we are not even sure (nor for that matter is she) she believes in; the essence of Quentin is to be fascinated by an incest he will never commit; the essence of Popeye, more or less independent of any given act, is nevertheless quite well defined by the corncob rape (impotence, sadism, and inhumanity all combined in one act), which does not at all exhaust his possibilities but which characterizes him and makes him exist in time.

Faced with these formulas, one thinks of Kant's "intelligible character" or of Sartre's "existential choice," which his version of the psychoanalytic method attempts to elucidate. But Faulkner's novels (unlike Stendhal's and Balzac's) are not intended to augment our knowledge of men. They are intended to communicate to us a certain version of the world, to make us share the fascination that is, in the final analysis, exercised on the spirit of man by a certain image of eternity, an "*Abbild*" that can only be situated outside of time. The very way he sees his characters helps impose that image. His revelations are not psychological but poetic. Even the characters' destruction is only subordinate; it is the inevitable obverse of the medal, cast in relief by Faulkner's work as a whole. He must of course deny the reality of the temporal, but only to affirm the eternal, in at least one of its aspects.

To "crush man," however, is perhaps only a subordinate goal for Faulkner. Behind all those beings he shows us as inexorably bound to one of their determinants (Popeye to his physiological defects, Christmas to his childhood of shame and misery, the convict to the sentence that juridically objectifies his past error, the doctor in *The Wild Palms* to the illegal love that has delivered him from his "bitter virginity," and so forth), there is nevertheless an outline (which they themselves may not recognize) of what is real in them—of what is beyond their temporal life and, though immutable, is not so in the same way as a prisoner's ball and chain—the great Eternal Act that constitutes their existence, the act that man can only contemplate if its image is pushed into the past, yet one that is essentially timeless. This is the analogue for the individual of what the Civil War is for the South or the arrival of the Pilgrim Fathers for the North American continent, or the two conjoined acts of the Creation and the Fall for Man in general.

Like the Jews of the Old Testament or the Negroes of the Southern plantations (the anonymous and collective authors of the spirituals), all of Faulkner's characters are turned to the past; they are busy reexamining the great immobile Event that hangs heavy over their heads and has made, so to speak, a hole in the monotonous succession of similar days without, however, ever managing to integrate itself into them—the captivity in Babylon contemplated in the Psalms and by the Prophets, or the Civil War, the events of which are endlessly repeated by the Sartorises and the Compsons. And it can in no way be different until, with the Incarnation—the Event that makes a hole in Time once and for all and yet never stops happening, destined to remain eternally present from the moment in which it happens—the marriage of Time and Eternity takes place.

It is no accident that I have so often mentioned Balzac and Proust or referred to the Old Testament in relation to Faulkner. His work—like Joyce's *Ulysses* and Eliot's poems, including *The Waste Land* and up to *Ash Wednesday* (the beginning of Redemption)—is a manifestation of the widespread malady of the modern spirit. This malady is to live in the time before the birth of Christ and thus to find oneself in the same situation as that of the entire Jewish people. It is easy to understand why the collective destiny of the Jews should have seemed so exemplary to Bloy, Péguy, and Maritain; and it is surely neither an accident nor an act of homage to Victor Bérard's theories about the Phoenician origins of the *Odyssey* that Joyce used a member of the chosen people for his modern equivalent of the King of Ithaca. This same malediction (as in the case of Joyce and of Balzac) is undoubtedly responsible for Faulkner's almost unconsciously adopting, with regard to his creations, the position that is traditionally that of God the Father.

We seem here to be very far indeed from the contemporary American novel. I ask only that one observe the curious and unconscious symmetry of the two greatest authors of the age we are here concerned with in regard to the conception of time that inwardly rules their work: the time of Dos Passos, whose novels are attuned to objective, cosmic time, which presides over the calendar, the tides, the waves of economic inflation or depression—in short, a time defined in *Timaeus* as the *mobile* image of eternity; and the time that Faulkner raises above his characters like an *"in hoc signo vinces"* banner, without them, however, being immersed in it—the *immobile* image of eternity, in which retrospection becomes the ersatz of an impossible contemplation.

CONCLUSION

10 *The Age of the American Novel*

Pray for us now and at the hour of our birth.

—T. S. ELIOT

In the United States it is a commonplace to say (in a disillusioned tone): "All American novelists die young." Of course they do not all succumb, in the biological sense of the term, to premature death—though that did happen, for example, to Nathanael West, author of the remarkable *Miss Lonely-hearts*, killed at thirty-six in an automobile accident; and to F. Scott Fitzgerald, the figurehead of the young literature of the twenties, dead at forty-five of nervous exhaustion (and, one is tempted to add, of despair), who left us, besides that extraordinary novel of the magnetic and maleficent power of money, *The Great Gatsby*, the detailed record of his spiritual and moral breakdown in *The Crack Up*; and to Thomas Wolfe, indefatigable writer, carried away at thirty-eight by a brain tumor that left him no time to make his writings into a truly personal expression and to master the deluge of words that flowed from his pen. Many talented writers begin brilliantly, with a remarkable book, then succumb to alcohol, to Hollywood life, perhaps to an even more profound ill. Such seems to have been the case of John O'Hara, author of the admirable *Appointment in Samarra*—whose two subsequent

225

novels, *Butterfield 8* and *Hope of Heaven*, were so disappoint-
ing and about whom one may say that from then on he out-
lived himself—and of Carson McCullers, whose first book,
The Heart Is a Lonely Hunter, remains her masterpiece.

Faced with these destinies, equally tragic whether they
be spectacular or dreary, we are reminded of the end of
"Animula," the terrifying poem—which cannot be read without a shudder—in which Eliot sums up human destiny:

> Pray for Guiterriez, avid of speed and power,
> For Boudin, blown to pieces,
> For this one who made a great fortune,
> And that one who went his own way.
> Pray for Floret, by the boarhound slain
>   between the yew trees,
> Pray for us now and at the hour of our birth.[1]

And it is interesting to note that the miserable ends of West,
Fitzgerald, and O'Hara were in a sense foreshadowed by the
defeat and failure of their three heroes, Miss Lonelyhearts,
the Great Gatsby, and Julian English—all finally overwhelmed
by the world they had hoped to dominate and transform.

The causes of this impressive "child mortality" among
American novelists are multiple and complex. The first is the
fact that the writer does not have the advantage of a long and
solid cultural tradition he can draw strength from in his fight
against the society that presses in on him from all sides. The
only more or less permanent tradition is that of New England,
but being narrow and puritanical, even provincial, it could
not furnish even Henry James or T. S. Eliot (who came from
this background) with the nourishment or the roots that they
both needed and finally found in England. Physically a small
area, reserved to a particular caste (to such an extent that
many well-known writers were never part of it), it was even

[1] T. S. Eliot, *Collected Poems: 1909–1962.* Reprinted by permission
of Harcourt Brace Jovanovich, Inc.—Tr.

in the last century so insular, so profoundly moralistic, so uncomprehending of aesthetic or spiritual values, that it was responsible for the artistic isolation of Melville and Hawthorne, both of whom were obliged to dissimulate their messages behind the veil of allegory.

In addition, the writer's public is neither stable nor homogeneous, and it remains, whether he writes for three million anonymous readers or for the New York intelligentsia, at the mercy of every passing fad. Dos Passos, in the article he wrote about Fitzgerald on the occasion of the latter's death, made a point of commenting on the difficult situation of the American writer, who knows neither for whom he is writing nor what level of awareness and intelligence he can count on his reader having. Previously, the Bible had provided for all those who knew how to read and write a common cultural background, a reservoir of themes and allusions understandable by all; in addition, because of its inner complexity and its archaism, it obliged the reader to make an imaginative effort similar to that which the study of Latin and Greek forced on the children of the rich. Now, as Dos Passos pointed out, the common background is the exclusively visual and auditory culture of the movies, which is not at all literary. In reaction to this, upholders of culture and champions of tradition tend to be aggressively reactionary and of a conservative temper, which is what Lionel Trilling once deplored about one of Van Wyck Brooks's books consecrated to the study of nineteenth-century American literature. The American writer is ultimately forced to choose between an audience of illiterates and one of puritanical professors, yet neither vast printings nor the approbation of intellectuals can reassure or satisfy him.

Though American novelists are admired (somewhat superficially) for their technical subtlety, they themselves wish to return to simpler, more archaic narrative methods. *Boston Adventure*, Jean Stafford's first novel, unfolds its story in a way that is reminiscent of Dickens and Proust, and the authors currently most in vogue are Melville and Henry James. At the beginning of this book, I discussed at great length the inspired, artful application of the techniques of the film to the American novel; when Dos Passos, the originator of "the Camera Eye," wished to award Fitzgerald the supreme compliment, he said that the latter (in his last, unfinished novel), instead of limiting himself to lighting his characters scantily from either above or below, was about to succeed in inventing a group of people that could be seen from all sides at once. The story of Naboth's vineyard might well have at its core an enduring truth. The most adventurous critics say they are tired of the descriptive method: they do not see reportage as literature, and they plunge with delight into Joyce and Kafka, Mann and Proust—in short, into structured, architectural works, more ample than the impressionistic works of immediacy that are—at best—excellent *New Yorker* stories but not enduring novels with multiple levels of meaning. The "age of the American novel" may well already be over in America.

It is also worth noting that the literature of the United States, especially fiction, seems to be suffering from a kind of aridity since World War II. Men and books alike seem strikingly short-winded. The works of the most gifted writers rarely exceed novella length; Katherine Anne Porter is a striking example of this. In addition, it is significant that the most successful works so quickly turn sour, contrasting their acidity with the national optimism of the magazines and digests. It is as if to be a writer in the United States is necessarily to be unhappy, if not despairing; as if the intellectuals truly constituted a sacrificial caste, predestined to sad lucidity, preordained to compensate, to expiate, the refusal of the rest of the country to recognize the reality of evil. Even those writers who seem by temperament to be the most optimistic, the most superficial, are gradually overtaken by bitterness. This can be seen in Ring Lardner's last collection, *The Love Nest*, of which H. L. Mencken notes the growing acidity and which, recalling the analogous change that took place even in Sinclair Lewis, he explains by saying that it seems difficult, even for an American, to contemplate Americans without giving way to something that must be called moral indignation.

It is to the novelists—Fitzgerald, West, O'Hara—that has fallen the task of showing us the two Americas side by side: the America of refrigerators, white telephones, and country clubs, God's Own Country, the America of the magazine articles and of Hollywood—and then the other one, the one that does not appear in the statistics or in the photographs: the country of despair, of groundswells of insecurity and boredom, of people who have "everything to make them happy," yet who commit suicide (like Julian English, O'Hara's hero) or who can only find existence bearable by dint of getting drunk every night; the America of the novels about the blacks and the "poor whites"; the America of Caldwell, Carson McCullers, and Faulkner.

It is perhaps especially from this point of view that the situation of the American novel is exemplary and that one can truly define our epoch as "the age of the American novel." Its interest for us comes less from what it can teach us by its technique and its preoccupations than from the fact that it illuminates a general condition that is currently also a condition of literature. I have already noted the words of Walter Rathenau, cited in 1941 by Gide, who discovered in them a still-fresh reality: "America has no soul, has not deserved to have one, for she has not yet deigned to plunge into the abyss of suffering and sin." In the nineteenth century, Crèvecoeur, Thoreau, Emerson, and Whitman refused to see this abyss; Hawthorne and Melville (and perhaps Poe indirectly and James timidly) were the only ones to explore it. But in Caldwell or Faulkner it opens before us as a yawning chasm. Now literature must do more than open the public's eyes and make it acknowledge the Devil's part in the world: the writer must not only be the scapegoat of a society, the expiatory victim who is appointed to lucidity and who purchases at the price of his own insomnia and neuroses the tranquil obliviousness of other men; he must also rebuild—or at least try to rebuild—a Church, and present us with an image of what this Church might be.

If Faulkner's work so surpasses that of all his contemporaries, it is not by virtue of its literary graces, technical perfection, or psychological acuity. It is because he is the only one to show us, in *Sanctuary, Pylon, Light in August* (to take the three novels in which it is most obvious), the reconstitution of a community that can truly be called sacred, of a "communion of sinners" cemented by a revertibility of merits, which does not the less exist because it is not consciously felt by either the characters or the author himself—or, to use more secular language, of a group of beings indissolubly bound because they all assume the same sin, committed by one of them; expiate it in their various ways, according to their own natures; and, consequently, find themselves on the way to Salvation. The obvious absurdity of Faulkner's plots, which everyone acknowledges, is only the obverse of this mystical, noncausal, nonpsychological participation in one community, the community of Sin.

In *Sanctuary*, the crime, under the double aspect of murder (Tommy's) and sacrilege (the corncob rape), is actually committed by Popeye; and it is as jealously screened from us, in terms of its material reality, as is in every religion the exact nature of Original Sin, which is always carefully hidden under the veil of myth because its precise form is essentially anecdotal and irrelevant. But none of the other characters is innocent of the crime either, not even the victim Temple, not even the well-meaning spectator Horace. All will be bathed in the blood of Tommy, Temple, Goodwin, and, finally, the murderer Popeye—the instrument of the crime, the scapegoat who has taken it upon himself to commit the Sin and who will expiate it in ways that will seem absurd or ridiculous only if one compares them with the ways of human justice.

The "fascination" that binds each of the characters to the others, as well as binding the reader to them and enabling him to participate in their communion, merely expresses the fact that they have all taken upon themselves the burden of the sin. In *Pylon*, Roger Schumann's blood will redeem the others (including the anonymous reporter); in *Light in August*, Christmas's blood will. In *The Sound and the Fury*, the sin is more complex, apportioned as it is among the various characters and not pertaining exclusively to any of them, whether it be Caddy's profligacy, Quentin's incestuous love and suicide, Jason's avaricious hate, or Benjy's castration. The same is true in *Absalom, Absalom!* All the negative conditions required for the construction of a Church are there: a corresponding communion of saints can be built on the communion of sinners. The same kind of thing is to be found in Graham Greene's *Brighton Rock*, for example.[2] What is distinctive about Faulkner is that this structure, common to all his novels, is each time formed anew, almost without his knowledge and certainly without any expressly theological speculation—whereas the work of Bernanos, for example, is openly, often obviously, based on religious meditation.

If Faulkner is so different from other American novelists

[2] A comparison of this novel with *Sanctuary* proves illuminating. Among the obvious similarities, I will note only the way in which the Sin (Hale's death, Temple's profanation) is veiled from the reader's knowledge in both books; the localization of Evil in two beings who rather resemble each other (in terms of their cruelty and impotence, among other things); and the theme of violated and despoiled virginity, which is to be found in Greene's other works as well.

who are his contemporaries, if he belongs—beyond time or period—to the company of Melville, Graham Greene, and Bernanos rather than to that of Caldwell (who like him speaks of the South) or Dos Passos (who like him dislocates the traditional technique of the novel), it is because he is the only one among them to have acted out, in all its fullness, the literary drama of the age—the reconstruction of a Church. Others have stumbled over the same problem (O'Hara, Nathanael West, Fitzgerald, and even Dos Passos), but in the end their Church disintegrates and the guilty one is excommunicated, left alone with his sin, while the other characters return to their pharisaical existences and believe themselves to have no part in Evil: Julian English commits suicide, the Great Gatsby expiates by his death the crime of another, and Miss Lonelyhearts does not manage to alleviate by one iota the weight of human suffering (on the contrary, he aggravates it by the least of his acts). In Dos Passos's *Adventures of a Young Man* and *Number One* Glenn Spotswood and his brother Tyler meet with, respectively, death and failure. Not one of these people has managed to integrate himself into the world, to make a connection with other people. The human tide sweeps indifferently over their fate, which has remained an individual one. America will not be saved. In Faulkner's work, however, the conditions for salvation are now set down, though it is a salvation that must still be worked out and will always have to be rewon.

Index

233